THE PRESIDENT

HIS DUTIES, RIGHTS, POWERS, AND RESTRICTIONS

(in the words of the Constitution)

In General

The executive power shall be vested in a President of the United States. He shall take care that the laws be faithfully executed.

The President shall be Commander-in-Chief of the Army and Navy of the United States, and of the militia of the several states when called into the actual service of the United States.

Compensation which the President shall, at stated times, receive for his services shall neither be increased nor diminished during the period for which he shall have been elected, and he shall not receive within that period any other emolument from the United States or any state.

Specific Duties of the President

The President shall from time to time give to the Congress information of the state of the Union, and recommend to their consideration such measures as he shall judge necessary and expedient.

Every bill which shall have passed the House of Representatives and the Senate shall, before it becomes a law, be presented to the President of the United States. If he approves, he shall sign it, but if not, he shall return it with his objections to that House in whic[illegible] originated. If, after reconside[illegible] proved by two-thirds of that H[illegible] other House, it shall become a l[illegible] shall not be returned by the Pr[illegible] ten days (Sundays excepted) aft[illegible] been presented to him, the same [illegible] in like manner as if he had signed [illegible] Congress by their adjournment prevents its return, in which case it shall not be a law.

Every order, resolution, or vote to which the concurrence of the Senate and the House of Representatives may be necessary (except on a question of adjournment) shall be presented to the President of the United States, and before the same shall take effect, shall be approved by him or, being disapproved by him, shall be repassed by two-thirds of the Senate and House of Representatives, according to the rules and limitations prescribed in the case of a bill.

The President shall commission all the officers of the United States. He shall receive ambassadors and other public ministers.

Sole Powers of the President

The President shall have the power to grant reprieves and pardons for offenses against the United States, except in cases of impeachment.

The President may require the opinion, in writing, of the principal officer in each of the executive departments, upon any subject relating to the duties of their respective offices.

The President may, on extraordinary occasions, convene both Houses, or either of them, and in case of disagreement between them with respect to the time of adjournment, he may adjourn them to such time as he shall think proper.

The Pre[illegible] ve power to fill up all [illegible] en during the recess of [illegible] commissions which [illegible] f their next session.

[illegible]ers Subject to [illegible] Sanction

[illegible] e the power, by and [illegible] advice and consent of the Senate, to make treaties, provided two-thirds of the Senators present concur.

He shall nominate and, by and with the advice and consent of the Senate, shall appoint ambassadors, other public ministers, and consuls, judges of the Supreme Court, and all other officers of the United States whose appointments are not herein otherwise provided for, and which shall be established by law; but the Congress may by law vest the appointment of such inferior officers as they think proper, in the President alone, in the courts of law, or in the heads of departments.

The President and Vice President

The terms of the President and Vice President shall end at noon on the twentieth day of January; and the terms of their successors shall then begin.

The President shall, at stated times, receive for his services a compensation which shall neither be increased nor diminished during the period for which he shall have been elected, and he shall not receive within that period any other emoluments from the United States or any State.

No person shall be elected to the office of the President more than twice, and no person who has held the office of President, or acted as President, for more than two years of a term to which some other person was elected President shall be elected to the office of the President more than once.

The 25th amendment to the Constitution provides that, upon a vacancy in the Vice Presidency, the President name a new Vice President. The nominee must be approved by Congress.

Qualifications for President and Vice President

No person except a natural born citizen of the United States shall be eligible to the office of President; neither shall any person be eligible to that office who shall not have attained to the age of thirty-five years, and been fourteen years a resident within the United States.

No person constitutionally ineligible to the office of President shall be eligible to that of Vice President of the United States.

Oath

Before he enter on the execution of his office, the President shall take the following oath or affirmation:

"I do solemnly swear (or affirm) that I will faithfully execute the office of President of the United States, and will to the best of my ability, preserve, protect, and defend the Constitution of the United States."

Facts About the Presidents

Forty-one men have held the office of President of the United States. Bill Clinton is called the 42nd President because Cleveland served two separate, unconnected terms, as 22nd and 24th Presidents.

Franklin D. Roosevelt was the first and only President to be inaugurated more than twice. Beginning with Eisenhower, the 22nd Amendment to the Constitution limits Presidents to two elected terms.

Theodore Roosevelt was the youngest President to assume office. He was 42 years and 322 days old on September 14, 1901, when he became President upon the death of President McKinley. Kennedy was the youngest man elected to the office, 43. Ronald Reagan was the oldest man elected; he was 17 days short of age 70 when inaugurated.

The mothers of twelve Presidents lived to see their sons fill the nation's highest office: Washington, John Adams, Madison, Polk, Grant, Garfield, McKinley, F.D. Roosevelt, Truman, Kennedy, Carter, Bush. The mothers of Washington, Adams, Madison, Polk and Grant were not present at the inauguration ceremonies. Truman's mother was living at the time he succeeded to the Presidency in 1945 but died before his inauguration in 1949. The mother of Franklin D. Roosevelt was the only mother to witness her son's third inauguration.

The fathers of six Presidents lived to see their sons become President: John Quincy Adams, Fillmore, Grant, Harding, Coolidge, and Kennedy. John Calvin Coolidge, notary public and justice of the peace, administered the oath of office to his son when he succeeded to the presidency on the death of President Harding, at 2:47a.m. on August 3, 1923, at the family homestead at Plymouth, Vermont.

The March 4 inauguration date fell on Sunday in 1821, 1849,1877, and 1917. The January 20 inauguration date fell on Sunday in 1957.

Monroe(1821) and Taylor (1849) took the oath on Monday, March 5. Hayes (1877) took the oath privately on Saturday, March 3, at the White House prior to President Grant's state dinner for him, and repeated it in public on Monday, March 5, at the east end of the Capitol. In 1917,Wilson took his second-term oath privately on Sunday in the White House, and publicly on

Monday, March 5, at the formal inauguration ceremony. In 1957, Eisenhower took his second-term oath privately on Sunday and publicly on Monday, January 21.

Washington, John Adams, Jefferson, Madison, and Monroe were members of the Continental Congress.

Twenty-three Presidents were elected to that office after having served in the U. S. Congress. Two Presidents served in Congress after the terms of office: J.Q. Adams in the House from 1831-1848, and Andrew Johnson in the Senate from March 4, 1875 to his death on July 31, 1875.

Eight Presidents had been Representatives: Madison, Polk, Fillmore, Lincoln, Hayes, McKinley, Ford, and Bush. Five Presidents had served only in the Senate: Monroe, Van Buren, Benjamin Harrison, Harding (a Senator when elected President),and Truman. Eleven Presidents were members of both Houses J.Q. Adams, Jackson, W.H. Harrison, Tyler, Pierce, Buchanan, Andrew Johnson, Garfield (elected to the Senate in 1880, but did not serve, having been elected President), Kennedy (a Senator when elected President), Lyndon Johnson and Nixon.

Andrew Johnson was the only President to be impeached. He was acquitted by one vote. A two-thirds vote was necessary for conviction; 35 of the 54 senators voted for conviction and 19 voted for acquittal.

Vice President Bush on July 13, 1985, was named Acting President of the United States for several hours in an historic transfer of authority from President Reagan under the 25th amendment to the Constitution. Reagan was having surgery.

Sixteen times the office of President has been held by a man who was elected even though he polled less than one-half of the total popular vote cast. The total popular vote includes votes cast for candidates of minor parties. The so-called "Minority Presidents": John Quincy Adams, 1824; Polk (D), 1844; Taylor (Whig), 1848; Buchanan (D), 1856; Lincoln (R), 1860; Hayes (R), 1876; Garfield (R), 1880; Cleveland (D), 1884; B. Harrison (R), 1888; Cleveland (D), 1892; Wilson (D), 1912; Wilson (D), 1916; Truman (D), 1948; Kennedy (D), 1960; Nixon (R), 1968; Clinton (D), 1992.

Birth and Ancestry

All the Presidents have been American-born. Those born before the United States became independent, in 1776, were Washington, John Adams, Jefferson, Madison, Monroe, John Quincy Adams, Jackson, and William Henry Harrison.

Born in Virginia: Washington, Jefferson, Madison, Monroe, W.H. Harrison, Tyler, Taylor, Wilson. Born in Ohio: Grant, Hayes, Garfield, Benjamin Harrison, McKinley, Taft, Harding. Born in states west of the Mississippi River: Hoover, Iowa; Truman, Missouri; Eisenhower and Lyndon Johnson, Texas; Nixon, California, and Ford, Nebraska.

Born in log cabins: Jefferson, Jackson, Fillmore, Buchanan, Lincoln, Garfield.

Sons of farmers and planters: Washington, John Adams, Jefferson, Madison, Monroe, J.Q. Adams, Jackson, Van Buren, Polk, Taylor, Fillmore, Pierce, Buchanan, Lincoln, Garfield, Benjamin Harrison, Coolidge, Truman, Lyndon Johnson, Nixon, and Carter.

Sons of lawyers: J.Q. Adams, Tyler, Taft, F.D. Roosevelt, Sons of ministers: Arthur, Cleveland, Wilson. Sons of businessmen or merchants: Hayes, Theodore Roosevelt, Hoover, McKinley, and Kennedy.

President W.H. Harrison's father was a statesman and signer of the Declaration of Independence, Andrew Johnson's a constable, Grant's, a tanner, Harding's, a doctor, Eisenhower's, a mechanic, and Regan's, a merchant.

President Bush's father, Prescott Bush, had been senator from Connecticut

The fathers of a number of the Presidents were engaged in two or more occupations; many of those listed as farmers or planters had other occupations.

Presidential relationships: John Quincy Adams was a son of John Adams. Benjamin Harrison was a grandson of William Henry Harrison. Taylor was a second cousin of Madison. Franklin D. Roosevelt was related by blood or by marriage, sometimes quite remotely, to 11 former Presidents: Washington, John Adams, Madison, J.Q. Adams, Van Buren, W.H. Harrison, Taylor, Grant, Benjamin Harrison, Theodore Roosevelt, and Taft. President Tyler's brother was the father of Truman's great-grandmother.

The lineages of most of the Presidents go back to the British Isles. Those of English ancestry: Washington, John Adams, Madison, J.Q. Adams, W.H. Harrison, Tyler, Taylor, Fillmore, Pierce, Lincoln, Andrew Johnson, Garfield, Benjamin Harrison, Taft, and Coolidge. English-Irish: Cleveland. English-Scotch: Grant. English-Scotch-Irish: Harding, Truman, and Reagan. Irish: Kennedy. Scotch: Monroe, and Hayes. Scotch-Irish: Jackson, Polk, Buchanan, Arthur, McKinley, and Wilson. Welsh: Jefferson. Dutch: Van Buren, Theodore Roosevelt, and Franklin D. Roosevelt. Swiss-German: Hoover, and Eisenhower. Lyndon Johnson was of English, Irish, Scotch, French and German ancestry.

Cleveland's baptismal name was Stephen Grover, Grant's was Hiram Ulysses, Wilson's was Thomas Woodrow, Coolidge's was John Calvin and Eisenhower's was David Dwight. The "S" in the name of Harry S. Truman is merely an initial or letter, and does not stand for a name. Ford was named Leslie King Jr., but later took his stepfather's name. Clinton was named William Jefferson Blyth, IV, but he took his first stepfather's name as well.

Many of the Presidents had no middle name or initial: Washington, John Adams, Jefferson, Madison, Monroe, Jackson, Van Buren, Tyler, Taylor, Fillmore, Pierce, Buchanan, Lincoln, Andrew Johnson, Benjamin Harrison, McKinley and Theodore Roosevelt.

Death and Assassination

Lincoln, Garfield, McKinley, and Kennedy were assassinated. John Wilkes Booth, the assassin of Lincoln, was pursued by soldiers, shot and killed. The assassins of Garfield and McKinley were legally executed. Lee Harvey Oswald, accused assassin of Kennedy, was himself, assassinated before being brought to trial.

Jackson was shot at, on January 30, 1835, in the rotunda of the Capitol, by a man who was later declared insane. The shots, fired from only a few feet away, missed the President. Theodore Roosevelt was shot in 1912 while a Presidential candidate of the Progressive ("Bull Moose") Party. Three weeks before his first inauguration, on February 15, 1933, F.D. Roosevelt narrowly escaped a shot fired by a madman, Guiseppe Zangara, in Miami, Florida. On November 1, 1950, in Washington, D.C., two Puerto Rican Nationalists made a futile attempt to reach President Truman to assassinate him.

Three Presidents died on the anniversary of the Declaration of Independence: John Adams and Jefferson died on July 4, 1826; Monroe died on July 4, 1831.

John Adams lived to the greatest age of any President: 90 years, 8 months. Kennedy was the youngest to die, at 46 years, 6 months. Eight Presidents died in office: W.H. Harrison, Taylor, Lincoln, Garfield, McKinley, Harding, F. D. Roosevelt, Kennedy. Two of these—Harrison and Taylor—died in the White House. Both Johnsons took office upon the assassination of a President.

Two unsuccessful attempts were made on the life of President Ford, both times by women.

On March 31, 1981, President Reagan was shot and wounded in an assassination attempted in Washington, D. C.

Education

Twenty-six Presidents have been college graduates: John Adams,Harvard, l755; Madison, Princeton, 1771; J.Q. Adams, Harvard, 1787;Tyler, College of Wiliam and Mary, 1807; Polk, University of North Carolina, 1818; Pierce, Bowdoin, 1824; Buchanan, Dickinson,1809; Grant, U.S.Military Academy, 1843; Hayes, Kenyon, 1842; Garfield, Williams, 1856; Arthur, Union, 1848; Benjamin Harrison, Miami University, 1852; Theodore Roosevelt, Harvard, 1880; Taft, Yale, 1878; Wilson, Princeton, 1879; Coolidge, Amherst, 1895; Hoover, Stanford, 1895; F.D. Roosevelt, Harvard, 1903; as of 1904; Eisenhower, U.S. Military Academy, 1915; Kennedy, Harvard, 1940; Lyndon Johnson, Southwest Texas State Teachers College; 1930;Nixon, Whittier College, 1934, Duke University Law School, 1937;Ford, Michigan, 1935, Yale Law School, 1944; Carter, U.S. Naval Academy, 1947; Reagan, Eureka College, 1932; Bush, Yale 1948; Clinton, Georgetown University, 1968, Yale Law School, 1973 (Rhodes Scholar.)

Five Presidents attended college but left before graduating: Jefferson studied at William and Mary from 1760 to 1762; Monroe left William and Mary in 1776 to become a lieutenant in a Virginia regiment; W. H. Harrison attended Hampden-Sydney, McKinley attended Allegheny, and Harding attended Ohio Central.

Twenty-six of the Presidents were trained in law and admitted to the bar as attorneys. Not all were graduates of law schools. Presidents who had no legal training or experience: Washington, W. H. Harrison, Tyler, Andrew Johnson, Grant, Theodore Roosevelt, Harding, Hoover, Eisenhower, Kennedy, Carter, Reagan.

Beginning with George Washington, many honorary degrees have been conferred by colleges and universities upon the men who have filled the office of President of the United States.

John Quincy Adams, Chester Arthur, Theodore Roosevelt, William Taft, and George Bush were Phi Beta Kappa Members.

"Firsts"

Early Presidents relied on horses for transportation. President Pierce, the first President to be arrested while on horseback, accidentally ran down a woman and was placed under arrest by a constable, but was released immediately. The only other President to be arrested - Grant - was exceeding the Washington speed limit while driving a spirited horse. Arrested by a policeman,

Grant put up a deposit of $20 and commended the policeman for doing his duty, but he did not appear in court.

Jackson was the first President to travel by railroad train while in office. On June 6, 1833, he traveled by the Baltimore and Ohio Railroad from Ellicott's Mills, Md., to Baltimore.

McKinley was the first President to ride in an automobile. In 1899, he was persuaded by inventer O.F. Stanley to take a brief ride in a Stanley Steamer. Theodore Roosevelt used automobiles frequently, for official and unofficial use. Taft was the first President to make regular use of an automobile at the White House.

The first official White House car was a huge, high-wheeled Brougham or landaulet, with folding top. During Taft's years in office, two other automobiles were bought—an open touring car to carry Secret Service men and serve as motor escort wherever the President's car went, and a luxurious limousine for state use. Harding was the first President to ride to his inauguration in an automobile.

Franklin D. Roosevelt was the first President to use an airplane for transportation during his term of office. After his term had expired, Theodore Roosevelt made a flight in a Wright Biplane on October 11, 1910, in St.Louis, Mo., on the occasion of an Aero Club meet. Eisenhower was the first President to use a helicopter. He was the first President who had been licensed to pilot an airplane.

Theodore Roosevelt was the first President to go down in a submarine. On August 25, 1905, at Oyster Bay, N.Y., he went aboard the Plunger, which submerged and remained under water about an hour. Truman was the first President to travel in a modern submarine. In Key West, Fla., on Nov. 21, 1946, he made a short trip in a captured German submarine submerged off Key West during naval exercises.

Eisenhower was the first President to submerge in an atomic-powered submarine, the Seawolf. On Sept. 26, 1957, he was aboard when she submerged off Newport, R.I., and remained 60 feet below the surface for 15 minutes.

Harding's election returns were the first to reach radio listeners—on Nov. 2, 1920, from KDKA, Pittsburgh, Pa. His inauguration was the first to be described to a radio audience. Coolidge's inaugural speech on March 4, 1925 was broadcast by 25 radio stations. Truman's inauguration on Jan. 20, 1949 was the first to be televised (to an audience of about ten million.)

Harding was the first President to make a speech heard by a radio audience, on June 14, 1922, at the dedication of the Francis Scott Key Memorial at Fort McHenry, Baltimore. F.D. Roosevelt was the first President to appear on television, on April 30, 1939, at the opening of the World's Fair in New York City. Truman was first to make a televised address from the White House, on Oct. 5, 1947.

Eisenhower's voice was the first to be sent into space by means of an orbiting artificial satellite; his photograph was the first to be "bounced" from earth to an orbiting satellite and back again. On Dec. 19, 1958, U. S. satellite SCORE transmitted his voice from outer space in a Christmas broadcast to all the world: "This is the President of the United States speaking. Through the marvels of scientific advance my voice is coming to you from a satellite circling in outer space. My message is a simple one. Through this unique means I convey to you and to all mankind America's wish for peace on earth and good will toward men everywhere." On Aug. 19, 1960, an Associated Press picture of President Eisenhower was shot 1,000 miles into space, bounced off orbiting satellite ECHO I, and received back on earth in less than five minutes.

Richard Nixon, the 37th President, was the first President to resign the office of Presidency as he faced impeachment.

Gerald Ford was the only President not elected to either the Vice Presidency or the presidency. He was appointed Vice President upon the resignation of Spiro T. Agnew in 1973, and succeeded to the presidency upon resignation of Richard M. Nixon on August 9, 1974.

Reagan was the first President inaugurated at the west end of the Capitol. He is also the first President who was president of a labor union. He was the first President who had been divorced.

Military Service

Fifteen Presidents saw no service in the country's armed forces: John Adams, Jefferson, Madison, John Quincy Adams, Van Buren, Polk, Fillmore, Cleveland, Taft, Wilson, Harding, Coolidge, Hoover, F.D. Roosevelt, Clinton.

Washington, Jackson, W. H. Harrison, Taylor, Pierce, Johnson (as military governor of

Tennessee), Grant, Hayes, Garfield, Arthur, Benjamin Harrison and Eisenhower were generals. Monroe was a lieutenant colonel and Theodore Roosevelt, a colonel; McKinley and Truman, majors; Tyler, Lincoln and Reagan, captains. Buchanan served in the war of 1812. Kennedy was a lieutenant, and Lyndon Johnson, Nixon and Ford lieutenant commanders in the U. S. Navy during World War II. Kennedy was retired from active duty (on reserve) as a lieutenant commander. Carter was a Navy lieutenant. Bush was a Navy pilot during World War II.

Religion and Affiliation

All the Presidents have been church members or have attended church services regularly or occasionally. Some attended services of more than one denomination. While in Washington, Presidents frequently attended services at churches other than their own.

Episcopalian: Washington, Madison, Monroe, W.H. Harrison, Tyler, Taylor, Pierce, Arthur, F.D. Roosevelt, Ford and Bush. Presbyterian: Jackson, Buchanan, Cleveland, B. Harrison, Wilson, Eisenhower. Unitarian: John Adams, J.Q. Adams, Fillmore, Taft. Methodist: Grant, McKinley. Reformed Dutch: Van Buren, Theodore Roosevelt. Baptist: Harding, Truman, Carter. Christian Church (Disciples of Christ): Garfield, Lyndon Johnson, Reagan. Congregationalist: Coolidge. Society of Friends (Quaker): Hoover, Nixon. Roman Catholic: Kennedy.

Polk, reared a Presbyterian, attended Presbyterian services regularly but did not join the church; a week before his death he asked to be baptized, and received the rite from a clergyman of the Methodist Episcopal Church who was called in. Hayes' parents were also Presbyterians. While a professing Christian, Hayes did not join any church, but after his marriage to Lucy Webb he regularly attended Methodist services with her.

Jefferson and Lincoln were fundamentally religious men but both disliked denominational divisions. Jefferson tended toward the Unitarian belief and Lincoln attended Presbyterian services, but neither affiliated with any denomination. Andrew Johnson is usually listed as a Methodist.

The following Presidents were Masons: Washington, Monroe, Jackson, Polk, Buchanan, A. Johnson, Garfield, McKinley, Theodore Roosefelt, Taft Harding, F. D. Roosevelt, Truman. There is contemporary, circumstantial evidence that Jefferson and Madison were Masons but their lodge affiliations are not known.

President Kennedy was a member of the Knights of Columbus, Fourth Degree.

Salaries and Pensions

The President of the United States now receives, subject to income tax, an annual salary of $200,000, payable monthly, plus a $50,000 expense allowance (taxable) which is to help defray expenses resulting from his official duties. In addition, he has up to $100,000 as a tax free allowance for travel expenses and $12,000 for official entertainment.

The Vice President receives $94,000 in annual salary, payable monthly, subject to income tax, plus an expense account of $10,000 a year, also taxable.

From Washington to Grant, Presidents received a $25,000 annual salary. By the act of March 3, 1873, the amount was raised to $50,000, and Grant received this in his second term.

In 1907, Congress authorized a presidential allowance of $25,000 a year for travel expenses. By the act of March 4, 1909, the salary was increased to $75,000. Taft was the first President to draw this salary plus travel allowance.

In June 1948, Congress increased the President's travel allowance to $40,000. In January 1949, applicable to Truman's second term, the salary was raised to $100,000 (taxable), and a second expense allowance was authorized to help defray expenses relating to the President's official duties—this allowance being $50,000 a year tax- free. In 1951, the Senate voted to tax the $50,000 expense allowance beginning in January 1953. The $40,000 travel allowance remained tax-free. The salary was raised to $200,000 during Nixon's administration.

The Vice President's renumeration has followed a similar upward course—$5,000 under the act of 1789, to $10,000 in 1873, to $12,000 in 1909, to $30,000 in 1949, to $35,000 in 1955. Since 1949 the Vice President has also had an annual expense allowance of $10,000, paid monthly, to cover expenses resulting from his official duties. This allowance was at first tax-free, but since January 1953 it has been taxable.

By act of Congress signed August 25, 1958 by President Eisenhower, an annual pension was for the first time provided for former Presidents. Upon leaving office, each President was to receive a yearly pension of $25,000, plus unlimited free mail privileges, free office space, and up to $50,000 a year for office staff. The first checks under this law were mailed on October 4, 1958, to former Presidents Hoover and Truman. The pension is now $69,630 and up to $96,000 for office expenses except for the first 30 months during which a former President is entitled to up to $150,000 a year for staff assistance.

There is no pension for former Vice Presidents.

In the past, $5,000 annual pensions for Presidents' widows had been granted from time to time by special acts of Congress, and a few lump sum payments made. The 1958 law provided an annual pension of $10,000 to widows of Presidents. The second Mrs. Woodow Wilson and Mrs. Franklin D. Roosevelt became the first widows to receive this pension. The pension is now $20,000.

By specific acts of Congress, the franking privilege (free postage) has been granted to the widows of Presidents.

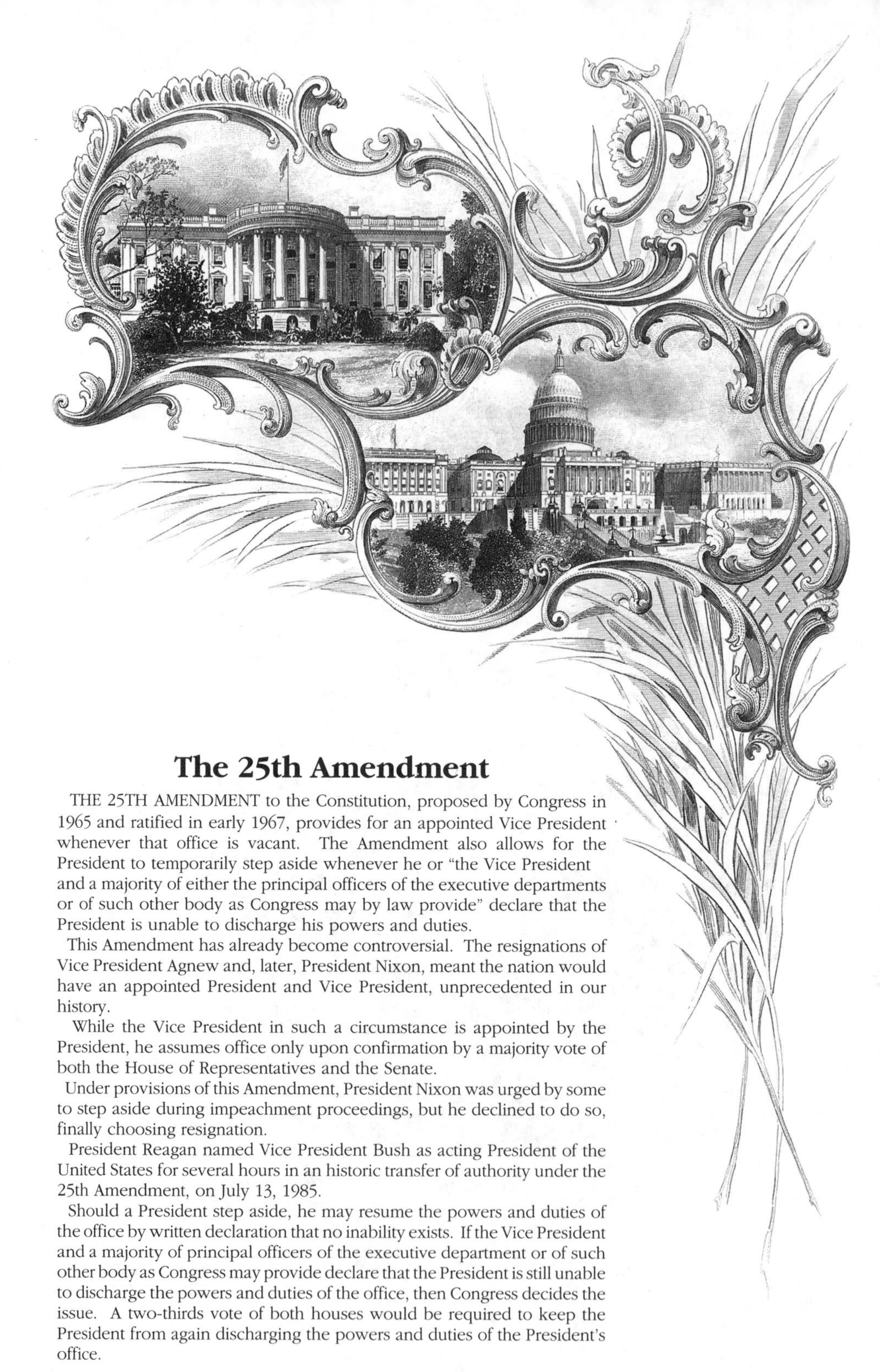

The 25th Amendment

THE 25TH AMENDMENT to the Constitution, proposed by Congress in 1965 and ratified in early 1967, provides for an appointed Vice President whenever that office is vacant. The Amendment also allows for the President to temporarily step aside whenever he or "the Vice President and a majority of either the principal officers of the executive departments or of such other body as Congress may by law provide" declare that the President is unable to discharge his powers and duties.

This Amendment has already become controversial. The resignations of Vice President Agnew and, later, President Nixon, meant the nation would have an appointed President and Vice President, unprecedented in our history.

While the Vice President in such a circumstance is appointed by the President, he assumes office only upon confirmation by a majority vote of both the House of Representatives and the Senate.

Under provisions of this Amendment, President Nixon was urged by some to step aside during impeachment proceedings, but he declined to do so, finally choosing resignation.

President Reagan named Vice President Bush as acting President of the United States for several hours in an historic transfer of authority under the 25th Amendment, on July 13, 1985.

Should a President step aside, he may resume the powers and duties of the office by written declaration that no inability exists. If the Vice President and a majority of principal officers of the executive department or of such other body as Congress may provide declare that the President is still unable to discharge the powers and duties of the office, then Congress decides the issue. A two-thirds vote of both houses would be required to keep the President from again discharging the powers and duties of the President's office.

GEORGE WASHINGTON, *First President*—April 30, 1789—March 3, 1797

BORN Feb. 22, 1732 (Feb. 11, Old Style) in Pope's Creek (now Wakefield), Virginia, of English ancestry. Son of Augustine Washington, a planter, and Mary Ball. A surveyor,soldier and farmer. An Episcopalian.

DIED Dec. 14, 1799, of laryngitis, at Mt. Vernon, Va.,age 67. Buried at Mt. Vernon.

MARRIED in 1759, Martha (Dandridge) Custis. They had no children.

Elections

1789 — Electora votes cast, 69. Each voted two choices.

George Washington, Va.	69
John Adams, Mass.	34
Scattering	35

Washington thus had a unanimous vote. Adams became Vice President.

1792 — Electoral votes cast, 132 Each voted two choices.

George Washington	132
John Adams	77
George Clinton	50
Thomas Jefferson	4
Aaron Burr	1

BORN on his father's plantation, the first President grew up near Fredericksburg and later at Mount Vernon, the plantation of his half-brother Lawrence. There he studied mathematics, became a surveyor, and later an officer in the Virginia militia. He served under Braddock against the French and Indians and attained military fame which brought about his selection (June, 1775) by the Continental Congress as Commander-in-Chief of the Revolutionary Army. After winning the war he sought to retire, but Virginia sent him to the Constitutional Convention, of which he was president, and he was unanimously chosen President of the United States under the new Constitution. He was re-elected without opposition in 1792, and refused a third term in 1796.

The whole organization problem of the new nation confronted him as President. He kept Thomas Jefferson and Alexander Hamilton as his Secretaries of State and Treasury, although they disagreed on political principles and had constant clashes about the building of a financial system, and army, postal and other services. European relations, federal court problems and the like were often solved peaceably only because all factions respected Washington as wise, just and fair. Washington City was founded but not occupied by the government until Adams' presidency, Philadelphia being the capital during most of Washington's two terms. He retired to Mount Vernon, but was recalled to Philadelphia in 1798 when war with France was expected, and devoted some time to reorganizing the army. He died, December 14, 1799, of a cold contracted while riding about his estates, after less than two days'illness. He owned vast estates in Virginia, and land given for his military services in what now are Kentucky and Ohio.

JOHN ADAMS, *Second President*—March 4, 1797 —March 3, 1801

BORN Oct. 30, 1735, in Braintree (Quincy), Mass., of English descent. Son of John Adams, a farmer, and Susanna Boylston. Educated at Harvard. A teacher and lawyer. a Unitarian.

DIED July 4, 1826, of old age, at Quincy, age 90. Buried in the First Unitarian Church, Quincy.

MARRIED in 1764, Abigail Smith of Weymouth, Mass. They had three sons and two daughters, the eldest son being John Quincy Adams, the Sixth President.

ELECTION

1796. Electoral votes cast, 138
Each voted two choices.

John Adams, Federlist	71
Thomas Jefferson, Dem.-Rep.	68
Thomas Pinckney, Federalist	59
Aaron Burr, Dem.-Rep.	30
Scattering	48

Adams was elected President and Jefferson Vice President

JOHN ADAMS, a prosperous farmer's son, was one of the early patriots, like his cousin Samuel. He signed the Declaration of Independence and served in the Continental Congress. A lover of justice, he endangered his life by defending in court British soldiers who, under orders, killed citizens in the "Boston Massacre." The Colonial Government made him its envoy successively to France, Holland and England. After freedom was won from England he feared the extremes of democracy, and favored a carefully limited form of popular goverment.

Elected Vice President with Washington in 1789 and 1792, he was the choice of the Federalist party to succeed the first President. Thomas Jefferson, the advocate of democracy, opposed him, and was named Vice President when Adams became President, the law then giving the offices to the first and second choices of the electoral college. Serious political strife marked his term, and a threat of war with the revolutionary government of France added to his problems. Toward the end of his term the capital was moved to the new city of Washington. Despite his long career of public service, he suffered as President from the fact that he followed the universally beloved Washington. He disagreed with many plans of his own party, which was led by Hamilton, and the opposition, led by Jefferson and Madison, grew stronger daily. When Jefferson defeated him for re-election, Adams refused to remain in Washington for the inauguration. The rivals became reconciled in later years, and from their retirement in old age each wrote advice to aid upbuilding the young government. Each died on July 4, 1826, fifty years to a day after they signed the Declaration. Adams passed away of debility and old age, the longest lived of all our Presidents.

THOMAS JEFFERSON, *Third President*—March 4, 1801—March 3, 1809

BORN April 13, 1743, in Shadwell, Virginia, of Welsh descent. Son of Peter Jefferson, a planter, and Jane Randolph. Educated at William and Mary College. A lawyer.

DIED July 4, 1826, of chronic diarrhea, at Monticello, his estate near Charlottesville, Va., age 83. Buried at Monticello.

MARRIED in 1772 to Martha (Wayles) Skelton. They had one son and five daughters.

ELECTIONS

1800 — Electoral votes cast, 138. Each voted two choices.

Thomas Jefferson, Dem-Rep.	73
Aaron Burr, Dem.-Rep.	73
John Adams, Federalist	65
C.C. Pinckney, Federalist	64
John Jay, Federalist	1

The tie result threw the election into the House, which chose Jefferson.

1804. — Electoral votes cast, 176.

Thomas Jefferson, Dem.-Rep.	162
C.C. Pinckney, Federalist	14

VICE PRESIDENTS: Aaron Burr of New York, 1801-1805. George Clinton of New York, 1805-1809.

JEFFERSON was a brilliant young lawyer of 33 when he sat in the First Continental Congress and was one of those chosen to draft the Declaration of Independence in 1776. Two years later he succeeded Patrick Henry as Governor of Virginia, and later the Colonies sent him as Minister to France. Washington named him his first Secretary of State, although Jefferson early displayed his opposition to the policies of the Federalist party, which was led by Alexander Hamilton, the Secretary of the Treasury.

When Washington's terms ended, John Adams, Federalist, defeated Jefferson, Republican, but the latter became Vice President under the electoral system of first and second choice. After four years his party won overwhelmingly in 1800, but the electoral college found Aaron Burr tied with Jefferson for President. The House of Representatives chose the Virginian. The twelfth Amendment to the Constitution, 1804, provided for separate voting for the President and Vice President.

Jefferson negotiated the Louisiana Purchase from France, adding the Missouri and half the Mississippi Valleys to the United States. He encouraged the Lewis and Clark Expedition to the Pacific Northwest, 1804-6, started the first national highway, to Ohio, established West Point, saw the slave trade abolished in 1805, and kept the new nation out of the Napoleonic wars, although our commerce suffered by the Embargo Act on foreign trade in 1807, which was modified two years later. His administration was marked by a naval war with Tripoli, in which Preble and Decatur distinguished themselves, and by Burr's filibustering scheme against Mexico in 1807. Fulton's first steamboat sailed up the Hudson, Ohio was admitted to the Union, and the westward rush of progress began.

JAMES MADISON, *Fourth President*—March 4,1809-March 3, 1817

BORN March 16, 1751, in Port Conway, Virginia. Son of James Madison, a planter, and Nellie Conway. He was the first of twelve children. Ancestry English. Educated at College of New Jersey (now Princeton). A lawyer. An Episcopalian.

DIED June 28,1836, of old age, at Montpelier, Orange County, Virginia, age 85, and is buried on his estate there.

MARRIED at Harewood, near Charles Town, Va.,(now W.Va.)
in 1794 to Dolley (Payne) Todd. They had no children.

Elections

1808. Electoral Votes Cast, 175.
James Madison, Dem.-Rep. 122
Chas. C. Pinckney, Federalist 47
George Clinton, Dem.-Rep. 6
1812. Electoral Votes Cast, ... 217
James Madison, Dem.-Rep. 128
De Witt Clinton, Federalist 89

VICE PRESIDENTS: George Clinton of New York, 1809-12, died in office. Elbridge Gerry of Massachusetts, 1813-14, died in office.

MADISON was one of the youngest of the Revolutionary patriots. He was first heard of as a great leader in the Constitutional Convention. He was the author of the "Virginia Plan," which proposed a goverment of three great departments—legislative, executive, and judicial—and furnished the basis for the Constitution of the United States as finally adopted. Elected to the first Congress, he there defended and interpreted the Constitution throughout Washington's administrations. With Jefferson and others he founded the Republican party of that era, whose principles were later those of the Democratic party. He fought for greater democracy, universal suffrage, state's rights, and less centralization of power. Jefferson made him Secretary of State.

Madison took office in the midst of controversies with England caused by that nation's blockades of France and her impressment of sailors from American ships when they were of British descent. England would not recognize our naturalization laws. This and other inroads on our shipping led to the War of 1812, which lasted until 1815 and was fought in Canada, in our northern states, on the Atlantic seaboard, in Louisiana and on the high seas. Madison was re-elected in the midst of it. Washington was taken and burned and the government fled into Virginia. In the long run American won a favorable peace. Two noted statesmen, Henry Clay of Kentucky and John C. Calhoun of South Carolina, were in Congress through these years. Madison's terms saw Lousiana and Indiana made States, Decatur triumphing in Algiers, the first protective tariff act, the United States Bank rechartered, Tecumseh beaten at Tippecanoe by Gen. William Henry Harrison, and John Marshall rendering his decisions as chief Justice which defined the scope of federal power.

JAMES MONROE, *Fifth President*—March 4,1817—March 3,1825

BORN April 28, 1758, in Westmoreland County, Virginia. Son of Spence Monroe, a planter, and Eliza Jones, a sister of Judge Joseph Jones, who sat in the Continental Congress. Of Scotch ancestry. Educated at William and Mary College but left to fight in the Revolutionary Army and was wounded in action. A lawyer. An Episcopalian.

DIED July 4, 1831, of old age at New York, age 73, and is buried in Hollywood cemetery in Richmond, Va.

MARRIED In 1786 to Elizabeth Kortright. They had two daughters, and a son, who died in childhood.

ELECTIONS

1816. Electoral votes cast, 217.

James Monroe, Dem.-Rep. 183
Rufus King, Federalist 34

1820. Electoral votes cast, 232

James Monroe, Dem.-Rep. 231
John Quincy Adams 1

VICE PRESIDENT: Daniel D. Tompkins of New York, 1817-1825

MONROE served in the Virginia Legislature, in the Continental Congress and the Constitutional Convention. He was one of his state's first Senators, was twice Governor of Virginia, was Minister to France and later to England, became Secretary of State under Madison, and then Secretary of War during part of the War of 1812. Washington and Adams, Jefferson and Madison, trusted and promoted him, and few men have served their country longer or better. He helped negotiate the Louisiana Purchase, and when he was President he bought Florida from Spain for five million dollars, with Spanish claims to the Pacific Northwest thrown in.

Monroe's terms of office were free from political strife and were called the "Era of Good Feeling." He was re-elected with one dissenting vote, a New Hampshire elector declaring that only Washington should have the honor of unanimous choice. He toured the North and West amid popular acclaim. Mississippi was admitted to the Union in 1817, and Illinois in 1818. When Missouri applied, the slavery question was raised for the first time. Under a compromise Maine came in as a free state in 1820, and Missouri a slave state in 1821, with certain limitations. The slavery issue was destined to remain in our politics until a bloody war settled it.

When he wrote to Congress in 1823, setting forth an American policy under which European colonization or interference in the affairs of North or South America would not be considered friendly conduct by the United States, he enunciated the "Monroe Doctrine" which has guided our statesmen to this day.

With the nation and most of the world at peace, Monroe's years in the presidency saw great strides in business, invention and western development.

JOHN QUINCY ADAMS, *Sixth President*—March 4, 1825-March 3, 1829

BORN July 11, 1767, in Braintree (Quincy), Massachusetts. Son of John Adams, second President of the United States, and Abigail Smith. Graduated from Harvard. A lawyer. A Unitarian.

DIED Feb. 23, 1848, of a paralytic stroke in the Capitol at Washington, age 80. Buried at the First Unitarian Church, Quincy, Massachusetts.

MARRIED in 1797, Louisa Catherine Johnson, of England. They had three sons and one daughter.

ELECTION

1824	Votes	
	Electoral 261	Popular:
John Quincy Adams	84	108,740
Andrew Jackson	99	153,544
W. H. Crawford	41	46,618
Henry Clay	37	47,136

There being no majority in the electoral college, the election went to the House of Representatives, which chose Adams. He received the vote of 13 states: Jackson had 7, Crawford 4.

VICE PRESIDENT: John C. Calhoun of South Carolina.

A HIGHLY educated man, who traveled much, John Quincy Adams was a fearless statesman and not always popular. He did not hesitate to change his political alignments, and was successively Federalist, Republican and Whig. Washington made him Minister to Portugal and then to Prussia. He served in the Massachusetts Legislature, and in 1803 entered the United States Senate. Resigning that post, he taught rhetoric at Harvard, was Minister to Russia under Madison, then Minister to England and Secretary of State under Monroe, negotiating the Florida Purchase and helping frame the Monroe Doctrine.

Party lines were forming anew in 1824 and the election was a personal contest. Andrew Jackson won the most popular and electoral votes of the four candidates, but the House, where the contest was thrown by lack of a majority , chose Adams. Jackson's following developed into the Democratic party, largely an outgrowth of the earlier Republican party of Jefferson. Supporters of John Adams and Henry Clay evolved into the Whig party.

The 1828 tariff bill set the highest protective duties then on record, and the South protested and advanced the doctrine of nullification, a forerunner of secession. The West was fast developing, spurred on by the opening of the Erie Canal. Adams was opposed to slavery and in favor of high tariff, government highways and internal improvements. He favored the United States Bank. Jackson's followers fought the latter as hard as they did the tariff. Adams was defeated for re-election, but soon was elected by Massachusetts to the House of Representatives, where he served until his death as an anti-slavery leader and a strong factor in the Whig Party.

ANDREW JACKSON, *Seventh President*—March 4, 1829—March 3, 1837

BORN March 15, 1767, in the Waxhaw district, S.C. Son of Andrew Jackson, a farmer, and Elizabeth Hutchinson. Of Scotch-Irish stock. Largely self-educated, he became a lawyer in Nashville, Tenn. A Presbyterian.

DIED June 8, 1845, of tuberculosis, at The Hermitage, his home near Nashville, age 78. Buried at The Hermitage.

MARRIED in 1791, Rachel (Donelson) Robards. Remarried, 1794. They had no children.

ELECTIONS

1828	Votes	
	Electoral: 261	Popular:
Andrew Jackson, D.	178	647,286
John Q. Adams, W.	83	508,064
1832	Electoral: 286	
Andrew Jackson, D.	219	687,502
Henry Clay, W.	49	530,189
Others	18	

VICE PRESIDENTS: John C. Calhoun of South Carolina, 1829-resigned. Martin Van Buren of New York, 1833-1837.

A PRODUCT of western pioneering, Jackson came to the White House after a career as soldier and statesman that included participation in Indian wars in Florida, defeats of the British at Mobile, Pensacola and New Orleans, personal duels, as well as service in Congress, and terms as governor and Supreme Court judge in Tennessee, and as first Territorial Governor of Florida. He had helped draft the Constitution of Tennessee in 1796, and came to the Senate at 30, to be made judge at 31.

This fire-eating duellist, fearless, self-made, and rough in manner, took his politics like his battles, and fought without mercy. Becoming President, he openly rewarded his supporters with offices, and declared that "to the victors belong the spoils," from which came the term "Spoils System." The system was not new, but the frank admission of it was. He would not compromise, however, on principle, and when Calhoun, the Vice President, advocated refusal by South Carolina to pay tariff duties, and talked secession, Jackson defied his partisan friends and declared he would enforce the law with an army if necessary. Calhoun resigned, and was sent to the Senate, where he and Hayne fought it out with Webster and the Whigs. Henry Clay, a Western Whig, effected a compromise, and secession was postponed.

Jackson fought the United States Bank and paved the way for Van Buren to set up the independent treasury. Westward and southern immigration brought on Indian wars — the Cherokees and Seminoles in the South, the Black Hawk War in the West. A young volunteer captain named Abraham Lincoln took part in the latter. Railroad building began. Arkansas was admitted to the Union in 1836, and Michigan in 1837, preserving the balance of free and slave states.

MARTIN VAN BUREN, *Eighth President*—March 4, 1837 - March 3, 1841

BORN Dec. 5, 1782, in Kinderhook, N.Y. Son of Abraham Van Buren, a farmer, and Mary Hoes. Of Dutch ancestry. Studied law in New York City. Member of Dutch Reformed Church.

DIED July 24, 1862, of asthma, at Kinderhook, age 79. Buried in the cemetery at Kinderhook.

MARRIED, in 1807, to Hannah Hoes, a distant cousin. They had four sons.

ELECTION

1836.	Votes Electoral: 294	Votes Popular:
Martin Van Buren, D.	170	765,483
Wm. H. Harrison, W.	73	739,795
Hugh L. White, I.-D.	26	
Daniel Webster, W.	14	
Wm. P. Mangum, W.	11	

VICE PRESIDENT: Richard M. Johnson of Kentucky, 1837-1841.

VAN BUREN came to the White House an anti-slavery Democrat, and remained such until he died. He wanted no more slave states admitted, and that question caused him to lose a few, and narrowly save other southern states in the 1836 election. On other issues he was with the mass of his party, although in Congress he had supported the 1824 and 1828 tariffs. The events of 1836 and 1840 foreshadowed the disruption of the party which occured in 1856.

The New York statesman had a long career as legislator, U.S. Senator, governor, Secretary of State and Vice President before he succeeded Jackson. He had also been named by Jackson as Minister to England, and sailed for London, but the Whigs in the Senate had refused to confirm the appointment. Public sympathy was with him and this helped in his choice for Vice President at Jackson's second election.

Coming to the White House, he was immediately confronted with a financial panic, 1837, surpassing any the nation had known. Speculation, the uncertainties about the termination of the United States Bank charter, and other factors entered into it. Van Buren was held to blame. He followed the Jackson program, and set up the Treasury of the United States independent of any bank. This plan was upset for a brief time in the next administration, but later was revived and has since continued. Van Buren was sound in his financial policy, but received little praise for it at the time.

He again sought the Democratic nomination in 1844, and in 1848 became the Free-Soil party nominee. Subsequently he supported the Democratic nominees, but remained opposed to the extension of slavery. He died during the Civil War, before the issue was finally settled.

WILLIAM HENRY HARRISON, *Ninth President*—March 4, 1841—April 4, 1841

BORN Feb. 9, 1773, in Berkeley, Virginia. Son of Benjamin Harrison, a signer of the Declaration, and Elizabeth Bassett. Attended Hampden-Sydney College. Studied medicine, but stopped to go west and fight the Indians. A soldier and a farmer. An Episcopalian.

DIED April 4, 1841, of pneumonia and pleurisy, at the White House, age 68. Buried at North Bend, Hamilton County, Ohio.

MARRIED, in 1795, Anna Symmes of New Jersey. They had six sons and four daughters.

Election

1840.	Votes	
	Electoral 294	Popular:
Wm. H. Harrison,	W.234	1,274,624
Martin Van Buren, D.	60	1,127,781

VICE PRESIDENT: John Tyler of Virginia, 1841.

GENERAL HARRISON, the hero of frontier days from the Ohio River to the Great Lakes, came to the White House at 68 years of age, and died a month after his inauguration.

A pioneer in the Ohio Valley, he became secretary of the Northwest Territory and later its delegate to Congress. He won early fame as a soldier, and when the Indian chief, Tecumseh, took the warpath, backed by the British, Harrison conquered him at Tippecanoe in 1811. The next year we went to war with England, and Harrison commanded the forces in the Northwest, leading the invasion of Canada. In 1816 he came to Congress from Ohio, and later to the Senate, resigning to be named Minister to Columbia.

In 1840 the Whig party held a convention and named Harrison after a contest with Henry Clay of Kentucky. One of the most spectacular campaigns in our political history followed. It was known as the "Log Cabin" campaign and the "Hard Cider" campaign, and Harrison's simple, pioneer life was widely heralded as a symbol of his merits.

The result was close in most states, but Harrison won all but a handful. Harrison chose Daniel Webster as Secretary of State, selected other able advisers, and prepared to restore the United States Bank, according to the Whig platform. One of his first acts was to call a special session of Congress. He did not live to see it assemble. Vice President Tyler, who took his place, did not follow his policies, and the Whig program was largely frustrated. Harrison's third son, John Scott Harrison, was in Congress when his father was President. A grandson was to be the twenty-third President.

JOHN TYLER, *Tenth President*—April 6,1841-March 3,1845

BORN March 29, 1790, in Greenway, Virginia. Of English descent. The son of Judge John Tyler and Mary Armistead. Educated at William and Mary College. A lawyer. An Episcopalian.

DIED Jan. 18, 1862, of a bilious fever, in Richmond, age 71. Buried in Hollywood Cemetery, Richmond Va.

MARRIED, in 1813, Letitia Christian. They had three sons and five daughters. After her death, in 1842, he married Julia Gardiner in 1844. They had five sons and two daughters.

Election

Was chosen Vice President with President Harrison, and became President upon the death of the latter.

VICE PRESIDENT: Office vacant during Tyler's administration.

THE Virginia Whig who followed Harrison in the White House soon developed as more Virginian than Whig. Tyler was never a respecter of parties, and always a deep student with finely drawn personal convictions. He had opposed Jackson, and as Senator had helped draft the resolution censuring that President for his handling of the United States Bank funds. When the Virginia legislature voted instructions to Tyler to withdraw the censuring vote, Tyler resigned rather than comply.

Tyler had served frequently in the legislature, been twice Governor of Virginia, chancellor of William and Mary College, a Representative and a Senator. Independence of thought and action marked his whole career. After Harrison's death, the Congress passed an act reincorporating the United States Bank. Tyler vetoed it. It was passed in amended form, and again he vetoed it, thus upsetting the whole Whig program. Unable to understand this from the man who fought Jackson on that issue, the Whigs disowned him. Tyler's cabinet, except for Daniel Webster, then resigned.

The annexation of the Texas Republic to the United States, and the construction of the first telegraph system, by S. F. B. Morse, were notable events of Tyler's time. Neither party considered renominating him, but a rump convention, largely of office holders, met in 1844 and offered to support him. He at first agreed, but in August declined to campaign, and retired to his estate, where he lived quietly until 1861, when he came to Washington and was president of the Peace Convention which tried earnestly to avert the Civil War. Its proposals failed, and Tyler returned home and joined the cause of Virginia; he voted for secession and was elected to the Confederate Congress, but died before taking his seat in that body.

JAMES KNOX POLK, *Eleventh President*—March 4, 1845-March 3, 1849

BORN Nov. 2, 1795, in Mecklenburg County, North Carolina. Son of Samuel Polk, a farmer and surveyor, and Jane Knox. Of Scotch-Irish decent. Educated at the University of North Carolina. A lawyer. Of Presbyterian ancestry, he attended services with his wife, a Presbyterian, but did not join a church. A few days before his death, at his own request, he was baptized by a Methodist Episcopal minister.

DIED June 15, 1849, of chronic diarrhea, in Nashville, age 53. Buried State Capitol Grounds, Nashville, Tenn.

MARRIED, in 1824, Sarah Childress. They had no children.

1844.	Election Votes	
	Electoral: 275	Popular:
James K. Polk, D.	170	1,338,464
Henry Clay, W.	105	1,300,097

VICE PRESIDENT: George M. Dallas of Pennsylvania.

THE rule of Democratic party conventions which required a two-thirds vote to nominate for the presidency had much to do with elevating Polk to that office. Van Buren expected and almost won the party support in 1844. When he could not muster two-thirds, the convention swung to the Tennessee leader. Polk had been legislator, Congressman and governor. For two strenuous Congresses he had presided as Speaker of the House. A brilliant orator, he was called "The Napoleon of the Stump." The 1844 platform called for admitting Texas to the Union, and resisting British claims to the Oregon Territory. Clay and the Whigs were less firm for these steps, and Polk won by a close margin.

Soon after taking office he sent troops to the Texas-Mexican border, which was in dispute, and clashes there led to war, declared in 1846 and pursued by our armies until they entered Mexico City. By the peace treaty in 1848, the United States received California and the area then called New Mexico (including Arizona and parts of Colorado and Nevada) for fifteen million dollars. At about the same time the Oregon boundary was agreed to, and the march of progress to the Pacific was complete. A few months after we gained California, gold was discovered there, and the rush began. Besides Texas, Iowa and Wisconsin were added to the Union in 1846 and 1848, respectively. It was an age of progress. Howe invented the sewing machine. Anaesthetics were introduced into surgery.

The first "tariff for revenue only" was adopted. The Free-Soil party was founded. Slavery remained a lively issue. Three months after his successor took office, Polk died at his home in Nashville, still a comparatively young man.

ZACHARY TAYLOR, *Twelfth President*—March 4, 1849-July 9, 1850

BORN Nov. 24, 1784, in Orange County, Virginia. Of English stock. Son of Col. Richard Taylor, a Revolutionary officer and Sarah Strother. Entered the army as a youth and remained a soldier. An Episcopalian.

DIED July 9, 1850, of a bilious fever, at the White House, age 65. Buried on his estate, near Louisville, Kentucky.

MARRIED, in 1810, Margaret Smith of Maryland. They had one son and five daughters.

Election

1848.	Votes	
	Electoral: 290	Popular:
Zachary Taylor, W.	163	1,360,967
Lewis Cass, D.	127	1,222,342

VICE PRESIDENT: Millard Fillmore of New York, 1849-1850.

LIKE HARRISON, the only other Whig to be elected President, Zachary Taylor was a soldier and later a farmer, and fought the Indians first along the Wabash. A Revolutionary patriot, his father settled early in Louisville, where Zachary grew up with a limited education. Once in the army, he advanced rapidly, won merit for gallantry in the Northwest and in Florida, and again in the Black Hawk War. In time he commanded the Southwest Department, and Polk sent him to Texas to hold the disputed bank of the Rio Grande against the Mexicans. Taylor held it, but war resulted. With inferior numbers, "Old Rough and Ready" won battle after battle, culminating at Monterey and with the overthrow of Santa Anna at Buena Vista. A grateful nation rang with his praises.

While on duty in Louisiana, Taylor had acquired a plantation there, and from there he was nominated for the presidency by the Whig party in 1848, just at the close of the victorious war. His popularity, coupled with the break of Van Buren from the Democrats to run as the Free-Soil candidate, helped carry the election. Another soldier hero of the West was in the White House, but, like Harrison, his term was never completed. He lived, however, to see another great struggle over slavery, this time about admitting California to the Union. The now venerable Clay, aided by Webster, worked out a compromise between the extremes, which once more delayed the final clash. California was allowed to choose for herself. She came in as a free state.

The Soldier-President had been in office sixteen months when a stomach attack seized him on July 4, 1850, and in five days he passed away. His death was part of the downfall of the Whig party.

MILLARD FILLMORE, *Thirteenth President*—July 10, 1850-March 3, 1853

BORN Jan. 7, 1800, on a farm in Cayuga County, New York. Of English ancestry. The son of Nathaniel Fillmore, a log cabin settler, and Phoebe Millard, a pioneer teacher. Of limited education, he was apprenticed to a tailor, but later studied law. A Unitarian.

DIED March 8, 1874, of old age, at Buffalo, age 74. Buried in Forest Lawn Cemetery, Buffalo, N. Y.

MARRIED, in 1826, to Abigail Powers. She died in 1853. They had one son and one daughter. Married, 1858, Caroline (Carmichael) McIntosh, widow of a prominent Albany merchant. They had no children.

ELECTION

Was elected Vice President in 1848, with Taylor, and became President upon the death of the latter. VICE PRESIDENT: Office vacant.

MILLARD FILLMORE advanced largely by his own efforts from a humble clearing in a new country to the White House, and while his career was perhaps marred by office-seeking propensities, he was considered a polished, accomplished statesman. Many details of his career were lost to history when all his private papers were burned by his son.

Starting without education, he was admitted to the practice of law at 23. He had already been in the legislature, elected by the Anti-Masonic party. He served four terms in Congress beginning in 1833. He wrote the tariff act of 1842. Defeated for Governor in 1844, he became Comptroller of New York, and won the vice presidency in 1848. Upon the death of Taylor, Fillmore endeavored to follow the latter's policies.

The gold rush to California was developing our western coast, and Oregon was asking for statehood. Fremont started exploring the Far West, and in a few years was to make himself felt as the first presidential candidate of a new party, the Republican.

In 1852 Fillmore sought renomination by the Whigs, but was defeated by Gen. Winfield Scott. Four years later he became the nominee of the American party, called the "Know Nothings," and made a lively campaign, but won only the electoral vote of Maryland. He resumed the practice of law in Buffalo, taking little part in the Civil War, and died of old age in 1874.

Three men who had done much in guiding the nation for a long generation passed away during Fillmore's administration: Calhoun in 1850, and Clay and Webster in 1852. Each had failed to be elected to the presidency.

FRANKLIN PIERCE, *Fourteenth President*—March 4, 1853-March 3, 1857

BORN Nov. 23, 1804, in Hillsborough, New Hampshire. Of English ancestry. The son of Gen. Benjamin Pierce, farmer, governor and officer of the Revolutionary army, and Anna Kendrick. Educated at Bowdoin College. A lawyer. An Episcopalian.

DIED Oct. 8, 1869, of stomach trouble, at Concord, New Hampshire, age 64. Buried in Old North Cemetery, Concord.

MARRIED, in 1834, to Jane Means Appleton of New Hampshire. They had three sons, none of whom lived to manhood.

ELECTION

1852.	Votes	
	Electoral: 296	Popular:
Franklin Pierce,D.	254	1,601,117
Gen. Winfield Scott,W.	42	1,385,453

VICE PRESIDENT: William R. King of Alabama. Died in office.

DISTINGUISHED, brilliant, unselfish and gallant soldier and gentleman, Franklin Pierce devoted much of his effort while President to preventing a final break over the slavery question, and was able to postpone the inevitable clash. Of all our Presidents, he alone went through his term without a change in his cabinet, a very able group of advisers.

The son of a Revolutionary hero, Pierce had Hawthorne and Longfellow for schoolmates. After service in the legislature and both Houses of Congress (he was the youngest U. S. Senator of his day) he retired from office and refused nominations for Senator and Governor, and declined Polk's offer to name him Attorney General. When war was declared with Mexico the already famous orator and statesman enlisted as a private. He was soon promoted and came out a brigadier general; at Contreras he had his horse shot from under him, was badly injured, but refused to leave the field. A compromise in the Democratic convention of 1852 brought his name forward on the 35th ballot, and he was chosen over Cass, Douglas, Buchanan and others.

Stephen A. Douglas offered in Congress the Kansas-Nebraska bill, allowing those territories to decide for themselves about slavery, and thereby repealing the "Missouri Compromise" and lighting the flame once more. Kansas was scarcely ever peaceful again for ten years. Pierce prevented secession, but harmony was impossible. During his term, Commodore Matthew C. Perry visited Japan and made our first treaty with that empire. The Gadsden Purchase settled our Mexican boundary. Pierce reorganized the diplomatic service and made a number of new treaties. His accomplishments, however, were not capable of pleasing either North or South, and he was not renominated. He traveled extensively in Europe in later years. Jefferson Davis was his Secretary of War.

JAMES BUCHANAN, *Fifteenth President*—March 4,1857-March 3, 1861

BORN April 23, 1791, near Mercersburg, Pennsylvania. Of Scotch-Irish ancestry. Son of James Buchanan, a merchant, and Elizabeth Speer. Educated at Dickinson College. A lawyer. A Presbyterian.

DIED June 1, 1868, of rheumatic gout, at Wheatland, near Lancaster, Pennsylvania, aged 77. Buried at Lancaster.

A bachelor.

ELECTION

1856.	Votes	
	Electoral: 296	Popular:
James Buchanan, D.	174	1,832,955
John C. Fremont, R.	114	1,339,932
Millard Fillmore, Amer.	8	871,731

VICE PRESIDENT: John C. Breckinridge of Kentucky, 1857-1861.

FEW men have suffered the criticism which has been heaped upon President Buchanan, near the close of whose administration the southern states seceded from the Union.

Buchanan had served long in both Houses of Congress, as Minister to Russia and England and as Secretary of State under Polk. His accomplishments were many. As a youth he had fought in the defense of Baltimore against the British. He became President of a bitterly divided people. His own party disintegrated into sections, a vigorous new Republican party rose, the Supreme Court in the Dred Scott decision upheld slavery, Kansas rejected statehood until she could have it without slavery, Minnesota and Oregon came in as free states, the South encouraged filibusters who promised to annex Cuba as a slave state, and John Brown staged his raid at Harper's Ferry. Buchanan sought conference and compromise. All about him was furor and action. The President strove to be right. Extremists on both sides were wrong, but they were strong.

The election of 1860 was a sectional contest, and the North united for Lincoln and won against a divided opposition. It was the signal for that secession which the South had threatened for many years. On December 20, 1860, South Carolina voted to leave the Union. In January, Mississippi, Florida, Alabama, and Georgia left. The rest left in February. The Confederacy was formed in a week. Its leaders seized federal property. Buchanan strove for peace, and the nation was at war. Fort Sumter fell. Lincoln came to Washington and took over the presidential office.

Buchanan had seen the panic of 1857, and the recovery. Silver and petroleum had been discovered in the United States. He had served long and faithfully, but the house fell about his head.

ABRAHAM LINCOLN, *Sixteenth President*—March 4, 1861—April 15, 1865

BORN Feb. 12, 1809, in a log cabin in Hardin (now Larue) County, Kentucky. Of English stock. The son of Thomas Lincoln, a pioneer settler, and Nancy Hanks. Self-educated. Farmer, ferryman, storekeeper, lawyer.

DIED April 15, 1865, the victim of an assassin's bullet. Age 56. Buried at Oak Ridge Cemetery, Springfield, Illinois.

MARRIED, in 1842, Mary Todd of Kentucky. They had four sons.

ELECTION

1860.	Votes	
	Electoral: 303	Popular:
Abraham Lincoln, R.	180	1,865,593
Stephen A. Douglas, D.	12	1,382,713
J.C.Breckinridge, D.	72	848,356
John Bell, Unionist	39	592,906
1864.	Electoral: 233	
Abraham Lincoln, R.	212	2,206,938
Geo. B. McClellan, D.	21	1,803,787

VICE PRESIDENTS: Hannibal Hamlin of Maine, 1861-1865. Andrew Johnson of Tennessee, 1865.

The tall, vigorous, simple Westerner who came to the White House in the nation's crisis of 1861 had served six years as a state legislator, 1834-40, and two years in Congress, 1847-49, but his fame rested largely on his debates with Stephen A. Douglas in 1858, where he sounded the keynote of the new Republicanism.

His inaugural address declared that "The Union of these States is perpetual." For a month, while preparing for war, he also pursued every effort at compromise. But the South had already seceded and formed the Confederate government and was making war. April 15, 1861, Lincoln called for volunteers, and on July 21, Bull Run was fought. Through four years he stood against all criticism, through disaster that preceded victory, firm for union. When the war required, he overstepped constitutional rights. Starting with no purpose to abolish slavery in those states already slave, he fearlessly issued the Emancipation Proclamation in 1863. Critics assailed him in the campaign of 1864, declaring the war a failure. He stood firm and won. He chose and encouraged generals, went personally under fire, sponsored the National Bank Act when the nation's finances tottered, called for a draft when man-power failed, and was kind and gentle as a child to those who suffered for the cause.

On April 9, 1865, Lee surrendered to Grant. Richmond was occupied. Victory was certain and soon to be complete, but Lincoln would not be there when Johnston surrendered to Sherman on April 26, or when the last spark of rebellion was quenched in Texas a month later. On the night of Friday, April 14, he was shot down while attending the theater, and died early the next morning. Stanton, his War Secretary, watching the tired eyes close for the last time, remarked, "Now he belongs to the ages."

ANDREW JOHNSON, *Seventeenth President*—April 15, 1865—March 3, 1869

BORN Dec. 29, 1808, in Raleigh, North Carolina. Of English ancestry. Son of Jacob Johnson, a sexton and constable, and Mary McDonough. Self-educated. A tailor.

DIED July 31, 1875, of paralysis, near Carters Station, Tennessee, aged 66. Buried at Greeneville, Tennessee.

MARRIED, in 1827, Eliza McCardle. They had three sons and two daughters.

ELECTION

Chosen Vice President on the Republican ticket, 1864, with Abraham Lincoln.

VICE PRESIDENT: Office vacant.

BORN to poverty in the Old South, Andrew Johnson was apprenticed to a tailor after his father had died rescuing a man from drowning. He taught himself to read, and organized a workers' movement which chose him alderman. Moving to Tennessee, he was elected mayor of Greeneville, where his wife, a teacher, instructed him in writing and arithmetic, and he debated with college students to learn public speaking. He served as legislator for four terms in Congress and two as Governor of Tennessee and went to the Senate in 1857 as a Democrat. He believed in states' rights on the slavery question but considered secession unnecessary and argued against it. When Tennessee seceded and he went home from the Senate his life was threatened, but he stood for the Union, and in 1862 Lincoln named him Military Governor of Tennessee. In 1864 he was named as candidate for Vice President at the convention of the Union Party, which was a coalition of Republicans and War Democrats. A month after the inauguration, Lincoln was assassinated and Johnson became President.

Immediately he sought to restore the southern states to the Union. In his impeachment trial he said his course was that which Lincoln had planned. He vetoed bill after bill, and Congress passed them over the veto, and devised acts to limit his power. Stanton demanded military districts and control throughout the South. Johnson removed him and named Grant. Congress denied the right of the President to remove a cabinet member, and the impeachment of Johnson followed. The Senate voted 35 to 19 against him, just short of the two-thirds needed to convict. On Christmas day, 1868, he issued a pardon to all who had taken part in secession. He remained active in politics, and in 1875 was elected to the Senate, but, after sitting in a short special session, he died in July of that year.

ULYSSES SIMPSON GRANT, *Eighteenth President*—Mar. 4, 1869—Mar. 3, 1877

BORN April 27, 1822, in Point Pleasant, Ohio. Of Scotch and English descent. Son of Jesse R. Grant, a tanner, and Hannah Simpson. Educated at West Point. A Methodist.

DIED July 23, 1885, of cancer, at Mt. McGregor, New York, aged 63. Buried in a magnificent tomb on Riverside Drive, New York City.

MARRIED, in 1848, Julia Dent of Missouri. They had three sons and one daughter.

Elections

1868.	Votes	
	Electoral: 294	Popular:
U.S. Grant, R.	214	3,013,421
Horatio Seymour, D.	80	2,706,829
1872.	Electoral: 366	
U.S. Grant, R.	286	3,596,745
Horace, Greeley, D. (Died Nov. 29)		2,843,446

Democratic electoral vote scattered.

VICE PRESIDENTS: Schuyler Colfax of Indiana, 1869-73. Henry Wilson of Massachusetts. 1873-1877. Died in office.

A man of few words if ever one lived, Grant was also a man of one purpose. Graduating from West Point in 1843, he was soon sent to the Mexican border, and in the following war was twice promoted for bravery at Molino del Rey and at Chapultepec. He was stationed for a time in Oregon and California until he resigned in 1854. He entered the real estate business, but was a poor businessman, and 1860 found him working in his father's store in Galena, Illinois, 38 years old and earning $800 a year. The Civil War broke out, he began recruiting volunteers, was made a Colonel and soon a Brigadier General, won minor battles in Missouri and Kentucky and then took Fort Henry and Fort Donelson, where he enunciated his terms "unconditional surrender." Promotion and higher commands and followed fast. In 1863 he took Vicksburg and Chattanooga, received the thanks of Congress, and was made Lieutenant General and commander of the northern forces. In 1864-65 he fought battles with Lee at the Wilderness, Spottsylvania, Cold Harbor and Petersburg, took Richmond and forced Lee's surrender at Appomattox.

Grant's selection for the presidency in 1868 was a popular choice and he seldom got on well with political leaders. He stood for reconciliation with the South, opposed inflation of the currency, dealt wisely with foreign problems and was re-elected. The political scandals of the time did not touch him personally, although some of his appointees were involved.

After leaving the White House he toured the world and in 1880 returned amid great plaudits, to be boomed for another term. He almost secured the nomination, but opposition to a third term prevailed. In business he suffered a severe failure in New York. He wrote his memoirs to restore his fortunes and provide for his family, working earnestly while suffering a painful cancerous affliction of the throat, from which he died.

RUTHERFORD B. HAYES, *Nineteenth President*—Mar. 4, 1877—Mar. 3, 1881

BORN Oct. 4, 1822, in Delaware, Ohio. Of Scotch ancestry. Son of Rutherford B. Hayes, a merchant and Sophia Birchard. Educated at Kenyon College. A lawyer.

DIED Jan 17, 1893, of heart disease, at Fremont, Ohio, aged 70. Buried at Fremont.

MARRIED, in 1852, Lucy Ware Webb. They had seven sons and one daughter.

ELECTION

1876.	Votes	
	Electoral: 369	Popular:
Rutherford B. Hayes, R.	185	4,036,572
Samuel J. Tilden, D.	184	4,284,020

VICE PRESIDENT: William A. Wheeler of New York.

Although remembered because of the remarkably close election which made him President, or because he was the first advocate of prohibition in the White House, or because the Treasury resumed gold and silver payments during his term, President Hayes was even better known in his lifetime for his war services and his efforts toward reconstruction in the South. His father had died a short time before his birth, but young Hayes was well educated through the aid of relatives, and was city solicitor in Cincinnati before the Civil War. In that conflict he rose to be a general.

He opposed, cut off and captured the Morgan raiders who invaded Ohio. At South Mountain he was wounded but would not leave the field until he fainted from loss of blood and was carried off. At the close of the war he was sent to Congress and then elected Governor three times.

The 1876 election found Tilden, the Democratic candidate, with 184 electoral votes and Hayes with 185 only if he won four contested states: South Carolina, Louisiana, Florida and Oregon. The voting in the South had been marked by many conflicts and irregularities about the Negro vote. In Louisiana it was charged that thousands of white votes were thrown out. The House of Representatives could reach no decision, and a law was passed creating a commission of five Representatives, five Senators and five Supreme Court judges, to settle the contests. This group included eight Republicans and seven Democrats, and decided every contest for Hayes by a vote of 8 to 7, and he won by the margin of one electoral vote.

Serious railroad strikes in 1877 disturbed the nation. In 1879 specie payments were resumed. The first silver bill was passed and silver dollars came in. Hayes made no effort for re-election, and retired to devote his remaining years to education and philanthropy.

JAMES A. GARFIELD, *Twentieth President*—Mar. 4, 1881—Sept.19, 1881

BORN Nov. 19, 1831, in Orange, Ohio. Of English descent. Son of Abraham Garfield, a farmer and canal constructor, and Eliza Ballou. Educated at Williams College. A teacher and lawyer. Member of the Disciples of Christ Church.

DIED Sept. 19, 1881, at Elberon, N. J., where he had been sent to recover from the wounds of an assassin who shot him at the railroad station in Washington on July 2, aged 49. Buried in Lake View Cemetery, Cleveland, Ohio.

MARRIED, in 1858, to Lecretia Rudolph of Ohio. They had five sons and two daughters.

Election

1880.	Votes	
	Electoral: 369	Popular:
James A. Garfield, R.	214	4,453,295
Winfield S. Hancock, D.	155	4,414,082

VICE PRESIDENT: Chester A. Arthur of New York.

BORN in a log cabin, his father dying when he was two years old, James A. Garfield worked for his education; he got it bit by bit when his savings permitted, but at 26 was a teacher of Latin and Greek and was studying law. He became a lawyer at thirty. Years later, after a term in Congress, he was still a student, going to New York to learn finance and banking.

Enlisting when the Civil War broke out, he attracted notice by leadership in the Western campaigns, and was sent to Washington with dispatches. Lincoln asked him many questions, found him thoroughly informed, and asked him to run for Congress and support the administration there. He reluctantly consented to leave the army, was elected, and put through the draft act and other war measures. The night Lincoln was shot, Garfield uttered in New York the famous phrase, "God reigns, and the government at Washington still lives." He remained in Congress many years.

At the Republican convention of 1880 he favored John Sherman for President, against Grant or Blaine. A deadlock ensued, and Garfield was the compromise choice, though he first refused out of loyalty to Sherman. The "Stalwarts" of the party, the Grant group, demanded a share of offices if they supported Garfield. After his election they were disappointed, and two leaders, Conklin and Platt, resigned from the Senate. The Vice President, Arthur, was a "Stalwart," and this fact may have been part of the motive of Charles J. Guiteau, a disappointed office seeker, who shot Garfield. Robert T. Lincoln, son of the Emancipator, was Garfield's Secretary of War, the only "Stalwart" in his cabinet.

His cruel, useless murder aroused world-wide sympathy and sorrow. He suffered for 80 days after being shot.

CHESTER A. ARTHUR, *Twenty-first President*—Sept. 20, 1881—Mar.3, 1885

BORN Oct. 5, 1830, in Fairfield, Vermont. Of Scotch-Irish descent. Son of the Rev. William Arthur and Malvina Stone. Educated at Union College. A teacher and lawyer. An Episcopalian.

DIED Nov. 18, 1886, of Bright's disease, in New York City, aged 56. Buried in Rural Cemetery, Albany, N.Y.

MARRIED, in 1859, Ellen Lewis Herndon of Virginia. They had two sons and one daughter.

ELECTION. Elected Vice President in 1880 with James A. Garfield.

VICE PRESIDENT: Office vacant.

The shock of Garfield's assassination, which made him President, also made Chester A. Arthur a decidedly stronger man of finer character than the politician of his earlier years. Historians agree that his administration was creditable, despite the political storms which preceded it.

His public services had been those of Inspector General and Quartermaster General in New York during the Civil War, and Collector of the Port of New York, a much sought political prize, under Grant. Hayes had removed him, and he was leader of the Grant third term boom in 1880. He was a lawyer of distinction, a leader of the Stalwart group of the Republican party, and opposed civil service reform. He was nominated for Vice President to placate his wing of the party, and six months after the inauguration he became President.

The Senators from New York had resigned in a quarrel with Garfield over the office of Collector of the Port, formerly held by Arthur. The Vice President had sided with them. Once in power, however, he sought to avoid partisan conflicts over offices, and was even partly won to civil service reform. Under many difficulties he strove to live up to the responsibilities of his office. The first Chinese Exclusion Act and the Anti-Polygamy Bill were passed during his term, and a new protective tariff. His party was weakened by its internal strife, and his Secretary of the Treasury, Charles J. Folger, was beaten for Governor of New York by Grover Cleveland. James G. Blaine resigned as Secretary of State, and in 1884 won the Republican nomination for President from Arthur.

President Arthur was a handsome, dignified man, courtly in his manners. Retiring to New York after his term ended, he died a little more than a year later.

GROVER CLEVELAND, *Twenty-second President*—Mar. 4, 1885—Mar. 3,1889
Twenty-fourth President, Mar.4,1893—Mar. 3, 1897

BORN March 18, 1837, in Caldwell, New Jersey. Of English-Irish descent. Son of the Rev. Richard F. Cleveland and Anne Neal. Educated in common schools. Became a teacher and then a lawyer. A Presbyterian.

DIED June 24, 1908, of debility and old age, at Princeton, New Jersey, aged 71. Buried in Princeton.

MARRIED, in 1886, at the White House, Frances Folsom. They had two sons and three daughters.

ELECTIONS

1884.	Votes	
Electoral:	401	Popular:
Grover Cleveland, D.	219	4,879,507
James G. Blaine, R.	182	4,850,293
1892. Electoral:	444	
Grover Cleveland, D.	277	5,555,426
Benj. Harrison, R.	145	5,182,690
J.B.Weaver, Peoples	22	1,029,846

VICE PRESIDENTS: Thomas A. Hendricks of Indiana, 1885-89. Died in office. Adlai E. Stevenson of Illinois, 1893-97.

The only President re-elected after a defeat

A SELF-MADE man, of great independence and courage, Cleveland ran for President three times and was twice elected.

He had been sheriff of Erie County N.Y., mayor of Buffalo and Governor of the state. As sheriff he personally hanged a murderer, refusing to give the unpleasant task to deputies. He fought corrupt political rings to the death. In his first term, as when Governor, he vetoed many bills, especially pension acts, and improved the civil service while his partisans clamored for the spoils of office. He opposed the silver coinage. After one term he was beaten by Harrison in 1888, although he won a popular plurality. The Tammany organization in New York opposed him. The Harrison administration passed the Sherman Silver Bill and the McKinley Tariff. In 1892 Cleveland did not want the presidential nomination, and his state opposed him, but the popular demand swept him into candidacy and into office.

A financial panic swept the nation, which Cleveland blamed on the silver bill, and he forced its repeal, selling bonds to maintain the gold standard. The Western Democrats reviled him. He opposed annexing Hawaii, sent troops to Chicago against a Democratic Governor's wishes to end the railroad strike and protect the mails, and denounced the "perfidy and dishonor" of Democratic Senators who opposed his low tariff policy. With similar fearlessness he forced Great Britain to accept arbitration of the boundary dispute between Venezuela and British Guiana, a step which established the Monroe Doctrine and the world power of the United States.

His party convention in 1896 refused to praise his administration, but eight years later his name was cheered in the conventions of both parties.

BENJAMIN HARRISON, *Twenty-third President*—Mar. 4, 1889—Mar. 3, 1893

BORN Aug. 20, 1833, in North Bend, Ohio. Of English ancestry. Son of John Scott Harrison, farmer and Congressman, and Elizabeth Irwin. Grandson of President William Henry Harrison. Educated at Miami University. A lawyer. A Presbyterian.

DIED March 13, 1901, of pneumonia, at Indianapolis, Ind., aged 67. Buried in Crown Hill Cemetery, Indianapolis, Indiana.

MARRIED, in 1853, Caroline Lavinia Scott. They had a son and a daughter. The first Mrs. Harrison died at the White House in 1892, and he married, 1896, her niece, Mary Scott (Lord) Dimmick. They had one daughter.

ELECTION

1888.	Votes	
	Electoral: 401	Popular:
Benj. Harrison, R.	233	5,447,129
Grover Cleveland, D.	168	5,537,857

VICE PRESIDENT: Levi P. Morton of New York.

PRESIDENT HARRISON, like the predecessors in his party, had been a general in the northern armies. A young lawyer in Indianapolis and reporter for the Supreme Court of Indiana, he early became a lieutenant of the 70th Indiana volunteers, rose steadily through meritorious and gallant services in the field, was made a Brigadier General in 1865. Returning to the law, he was active in public affairs, and in 1876 was nominated for Governor, but defeated. In 1878 he was named to the Mississippi River Commission, and in 1880 elected U.S. Senator, serving one term.

The McKinley Tariff and the Sherman Anti-Trust Bill were enacted in 1890, as was the Sherman Silver Bill, a measure blamed by some for the panic of 1892-3. A few years later the parties reversed their positions on the silver coinage. Harrison's administration also saw the first Pan-American Congress and the establishment of Sequoia and Yosemite National Parks. The Bering Sea Controversy with England and the Samoan trouble with Germany were peacefully adjusted.

North and South Dakota, Montana and Washington were admitted to the Union in 1889, and Idaho and Wyoming in 1890. The Oklahoma Territory was organized. The Dependent Pension Law doubled the number of pensioners of the Civil War.

Harrison was renominated in 1892, but despite the losses of the Democrats through the arising of the Populist Party and the solid support of the G.A.R., he was defeated, partly by reason of the financial panic which began in that year.

Harrison lectured for a time at Leland Stanford University, practiced law and was counsel for Venezuela in her boundary dispute with England. He represented the United States at the Hague conference in 1899, which was his last important public service prior to his death two years later.

WILLIAM MCKINLEY, *Twenty-fifth President*—Mar. 4, 1897—Sept. 14, 1901

BORN Jan. 29, 1843, in Niles, Ohio. Of Scotch-Irish descent. Son of William McKinley, an iron manufacturer, and Nancy Allison. Attended Allegheny College. A Lawyer. A Methodist.

DIED Sept. 14, 1901 in Buffalo, from wounds inflicted by an assassin, aged 58. Buried in Canton, Ohio.

MARRIED, in 1871, Ida Saxton. They had two daughters.

ELECTIONS

1896.	Votes	
	Electoral: 447	Popular:
Wm. McKinley, R.	271	7,102,246
Wm. J. Bryan, D.	176	6,492,559
1900.	Electoral: 447	
Wm. McKinley, R.	292	7,218,491
Wm. J. Bryan, D.	155	6,356,734

VICE PRESIDENTS: Garrett A. Hobart of New Jersey, 1897-99;died. Theodore Roosevelt, 1901.

McKINLEY had served in the Civil War, from private to major, had held local offices, between fifteen years in Congress, 1876-91, and was twice Governor of Ohio, 1981-5, before he was chosen President on the gold, or sound money, platform of his party in 1896. William Jennings Bryan, the brilliant orator, had swung the Democracy to a silver coinage policy, and was to lose the Presidency three times. McKinley's term saw a new protective tariff and the annexation of Hawaii, while trouble with Spain was brewing over the brutal treatment of the revolutionists in Cuba. Finally the U.S. Battleship Main, stationed at Havana to watch developments, was blown up with great loss of life. Spain was blamed, and we declared war.

Our navy was victorious in the Philippines, taking Manila, and at Santiago, destroying the Spanish fleet, and our forces landed and took Santiago, while another force took Puerto Rico. A young New Yorker, Theodore Roosevelt, commanding the First Volunteer Cavalry, a regiment of Western cowboys called the "Rough Riders," was a hero of the fighting on land. By the peace treaty, Cuba became a free republic under our temporary protection, and the Philippines and Puerto Rico were our possessions. These acquisitions, with Hawaii, and a part of Samoa acquired from Germany in 1900, gave us a new colonial problem and made us more decidedly a world power. In the Boxer uprisings in China our troops, with those of the European powers, marched to Peking and restored order in 1900. McKinley was re-elected in 1900, with Roosevelt as Vice President.

At the Pan-American Exposition in Buffalo, the President was shot twice, on September 6, 1901 by an anarchist named Czolgosz, and died eight days later. A period of mourning followed, and the President's body was taken in state to Washington, and later to his home at Canton, Ohio for burial.

THEODORE ROOSEVELT, *Twenty-sixth President*—Sept. 14, 1901—Mar. 3, 1909

BORN Oct. 27, 1858, in New York City. Of Dutch ancestry. Son of Theodore Roosevelt, a merchant, and Martha Bulloch. Educated at Harvard. A lawyer, rancher, author. Member of the Dutch Reformed Church.

DIED Jan 6, 1919, of inflammatory rheumatism, in Oyster Bay, New York, aged 60. Buried in Oyster Bay.

MARRIED, in 1880, Alice Hathaway Lee. They had one daughter. Mrs. Roosevelt died in 1884 and in 1886 he married Edith Kermit Carow. They had four sons and one daughter.

ELECTION

1904.	Votes	
	Electoral: 476	Popular:
Theodore Roosevelt, R.	336	7,628,461
Alton B. Parker, D.	140	5,084,223

VICE PRESIDENT: Charles W. Fairbanks of Indiana, 1905-09.

The youngest man ever to reach the presidential office, Theodore Roosevelt at 42 had been Police Commissioner of New York, Civil Service Commissioner, Assistant Secretary of the Navy, Commander of the Rough Riders in Cuba, and Governor of New York.

His outstanding act as President was to start building the Panama Canal. He vigorously fought trusts and monopolies. Congress enacted the first bill to irrigate the desert lands of the West, and created a new Department of Commerce and Labor. A new railroad act, inspired by the evils of rebates given to favored shippers, empowered the Interstate Commerce Commission to fix rates. The Alaska Boundary was settled, a pure food bill enacted, and the Japanese-Russian War settled by a treaty framed through Roosevelt's invitation, at Portsmouth, New Hampshire. Roosevelt, who had succeeded the martyred McKinley, was easily elected in 1904. With all his work, he was a hunter, horseman, and tennis player, and he kept the public interested in many things not official, such as his advocacy of large families.

He practically chose his successor, William H. Taft, but disagreed with him during his term, and sought nomination himself four years later. Losing to Taft at the Republican convention, he formed a new party, the Progressives, and made a lively campaign. Wilson, a Democrat, was elected, with Roosevelt second and Taft a poor third.

Roosevelt hunted and explored extensively in Africa and South America. In 1917 he asked permission to raise a division of troops for World War service, but it was not granted. He supported the war in unofficial ways. He wrote many books, and helped edit a magazine. An eternally active man, he died in his sleep, after a short illness, at 60. A popular idol, he had lived up to his famous slogan, "The Strenuous Life."

WILLIAM H. TAFT, *Twenty-seventh President*—Mar. 4,1909-Mar.3,1913

BORN Sept. 15, 1857, in Cincinnati, Ohio. Of English ancestry. The son of Alphonso Taft, who was Secretary of War and later Attorney General under Grant, and his second wife, Louisa M. Torrey. Educated at Yale University. A lawyer. A Unitarian.

DIED March 8, 1930, of arteriosclerosis, in Washington, D.C., aged 72. Buried in Arlington National Cemetery, Virginia.

MARRIED, in 1886, Helen Herron. They had two sons and one daughter.

ELECTION

1908.	Votes	
	Electoral: 483	Popular:
Wm. H. Taft, R.	321	7,675,320
Wm. J. Bryan, D.	162	6,412,294

VICE PRESIDENT: James S. Sherman of New York. Died Oct. 30, 1912.

Although Taft came to the White House at least partly by the support of President Roosevelt, he had a long record of exceptional public service. He had been Assistant Prosecutor and City Solicitor in Cincinnati, and Superior Court judge. He was Solicitor General of the United States, 1890-92, U.S. Circuit judge, 1892-1900, President of the Philippine Commission, 1900-01, Governor of the Philippines, to 1904, and Secretary of War, 1904-8.

His administration began with a special session of Congress to revise the tariff downward, as promised in the campaign. The resulting Payne-Aldrich Act was largely revision upward. A break between the conservative and radical members of the controlling party began. It grew over the question of preserving, or of selling, public lands, and Taft's Secretary of the Interior, Richard A Ballinger, was forced to resign. The "Insurgents" combined with the Democrats to upset Republican control in Congress, and two constitutional amendments, one allowing income taxes and one providing direct election of Senators, were among the results. A postal savings act was passed, as was a bill for trade reciprocity with Canada, but Canada rejected it. The Department of Labor was created, arbitration treaties were negotiated with many nations, and Secretary of State Knox proposed a permanent court of international justice at The Hague. New Mexico and Arizona were admitted to the Union.

Ex-President Roosevelt took up the Insurgent cause, and Taft was overwhelmingly defeated for re-election, retiring to teach law at Yale from 1913-21. He supported the American war effort, advocating a League to Enforce Peace somewhat similar to the League of Nations. President Harding named him Chief Justice of the Supreme Court in 1921.

WOODROW WILSON, *Twenty-eight* President—Mar. 4, 1913—Mar. 3, 1921

BORN Dec. 28, 1856, in Staunton, Virginia. Of Scotch-Irish ancestry. Son of Rev. Joseph R. Wilson and Janet (Jessie) Woodrow. Educated at Princeton. A lawyer and teacher. A Presbyterian.

DIED Feb. 3, 1924, of heart disease, in Washington, D.C., aged 67. Buried in the National Cathedral, Washington.

MARRIED, in 1885, Ellen Louise Axson. They had three daughters. She died in 1914, and he married Edith (Bolling) Galt, 1915.

ELECTIONS

1912.	Votes	
	Electoral: 531	Popular:
Woodrow Wilson, D.	435	6,296,547
Theodore Roosevelt, Prog.	88	4,118,571
Wm. H. Taft	8	3,486,720
1916.	Electoral: 531	
Woodrow Wilson, D.	277	9,127,695
Chas. E. Hughes, R.	254	8,533,507

VICE PRESIDENT: Thomas R. Marshall of Indiana.

The schoolmaster President came to the White House after 25 years of teaching and two years as Governor of New Jersey. Twenty years had he been at Princeton, teaching jurisprudence and political economy, and eight years as president of the University. He had written much on history and government. His term as Governor had witnessed important reforms. With a Democratic Congress, he reformed the tariff, enacted the Federal Reserve Law which reorganized the whole financial structure of the nation, and secured many other acts. He revived the habit of George Washington of speaking in person to Congress instead of sending messages. While his domestic plan prospered, he had trouble with Mexico, which was a scene of repeated revolutions, and with two brief invasions by American forces.

The World War broke in Europe, and Wilson called on America to remain neutral. Despite many difficulties, neutrality was maintained until 1917. In 1916, Wilson was re-elected in a very close contest with former Justice Charles E. Hughes, of the Supreme Court, as his opponent. In 1917 German attacks on our shipping finally forced us into the war. When it was won, Wilson went to Paris in person to sit in on the peace conference. The Treaty included the League of Nations Covenant, of which Wilson was part author and chief sponsor. Most of the nations of the world adopted it, but the U.S. Senate refused to ratify. Wilson was sent west on a speaking tour to win popular support for the treaty and was stricken with paralysis, returning to the White House an invalid.

Affairs during his remaining months in office were conducted largely from his wheel chair, but he kept a mental grasp of his tasks, and rode to the Capitol to see his successor sworn in. His great accomplishments and the winning of the war were for a time overshadowed by the failure of the treaty.

WARREN G. HARDING, *Twenty-ninth President*—Mar. 4, 1921—Aug. 2, 1923

BORN Nov. 2, 1865, in Corsica, Ohio. Of Scotch-Irish and English ancestry. Son of Dr. George T. Harding and Phoebe Elizabeth Dickerson. Attended Ohio Central College. A newspaper publisher. A Baptist.

DIED Aug. 2, 1923, in San Francisco, Calif., of pneumonia and heart trouble, aged 57. Buried in Marion, Ohio.

MARRIED, in 1891, Florence Kling. They had no children.

ELECTION

1920.	Votes	
	Electoral: 531	Popular:
Warren G. Harding, R.	404	16,143,407
James M. Cox, D.	127	9,130,328

VICE PRESIDENT: Calvin Coolidge of Massachusetts.

HARDING, like many of his predecessors since the convention nominating system began, was a compromise choice of his party, but he was elected President by the largest majority recorded to that time. He had been a newspaper worker and publisher all his life in Marion, Ohio, serving in the State Senate, as Lieutenant Governor of Ohio, and as U.S. Senator from 1915 until chosen President.

Early in his administration he summoned the allied and associated powers to a conference in Washington to consider steps which would stop the race of naval construction which had each nation arming to the teeth in fear of its neighbor. The plan of Secretary of State Hughes for limiting the size of navies was adopted, the first successful effort of the sort in world history. At the same conference a treaty was adopted governing the action of all powers concerned about their possessions in the Pacific Ocean.

The Republicans wrote a tariff bill along protective lines and enacted numerous laws necessary in restoring business to a normal, peace-time basis. Laws were passed to care for disabled soldiers, but Harding vetoed a general bonus for all who had fought in the war. A national budget law aimed at economy in government was put into effect. The Territory of Alaska had for years been asking for increased self-government, and the President set out in the summer of 1923 to visit the northland, making numerous speeches en route, and stopping on Canadian soil on his return. On his way back he was taken ill in San Francisco, and died there on August 2. A special train conveyed his remains to the capital, thousands of silent citizens watching it pass through the cities and towns en route. After a formal funeral in Washington, the President was buried at his home town - Marion, Ohio.

CALVIN COOLIDGE, *Thirtieth President*—August 3, 1923—March 3, 1929

BORN July 4, 1872, in Plymouth, Vermont. Of an old Puritan family. Son of Col. John Coolidge, farmer, and Victoria Moor. Educated at Amherst College. A lawyer. A Congregationalist.

DIED January 5, 1933, at his home in Northampton, Mass., of a heart attack. Buried in Plymouth, Vt.

MARRIED, in 1905, to Grace A. Goodhue. They had two sons, the younger of whom, Calvin, died in Washington, July 7, 1924, aged 16.

ELECTION

1924.	Votes	
	Electoral: 531	Popular:
Calvin Coolidge, R.	382	15,718,211
John W. Davis, D.	136	8,385,283
Robt. M. LaFollette, Prog.	13	4,831,289

VICE PRESIDENT: Charles G. Dawes of Illinois, 1925-29.

A TYPICAL, silent Vermont Yankee succeeded to the presidency upon the death of Warren Harding, when Calvin Coolidge took the oath of office by lamplight in the modest farmhouse of his father among the New England hills.

His administration was marked by a policy of rigid economy in government operations, and reductions in taxes. He vetoed soldiers' bonus and pension bills and other measures involving large expenditures and adopted a conservative attitude on most national problems. Some scandals which arose from the conduct of officials in the previous regime were offset by the high personal character of the President and the rigid integrity of his appointees. Toward the close of his term the appropriations for Mississippi River flood control, the construction of the great Boulder Canyon Dam on the Colorado River, and other developments somewhat offset his economic program.

In 1924 Coolidge was elected by a wide plurality over John W. Davis, Democrat and former ambassador to England, and Senator La Follette of Wisconsin, who headed an independent, progressive-socialist combination which carried only the state of Wisconsin.

Great material prosperity marked the Coolidge years at the White House. A treaty among all leading nations to forego war as an instrument of national policy was negotiated. Relations with Latin-America were improved by conferences and treaties. President Coolidge firmly declined to be nominated by his party for a second elective term in 1928, his presidency, therefore, covering four years to which he was elected and nineteen months of the Harding term. His refusal to be again nominated avoided raising the third term question.

HERBERT CLARK HOOVER, *Thirty-first President*—Mar.4,1929—Mar.3,1933

BORN Aug. 10, 1874, in West Branch, Iowa. Of Swiss and German descent. Son of Jesse Clark Hoover, a blacksmith, and Hulda Randall Minthorn. Educated at Stanford University. A mining engineer. A Quaker.

MARRIED in 1899 to Lou Henry of California. They had two sons, Herbert, Jr., and Allan.

DIED Oct.20, 1964, after a lengthy illness, in New York at the age of 90. He was buried at West Branch, Iowa.

Election

1928.	Votes	
	Electoral: 531	Popular:
Herbert Hoover, R.	444	21,391,993
Alfred E. Smith, D.	87	15,016,169

VICE PRESIDENT: Charles Curtis of Kansas.

The first engineer President, Hoover was the most widely traveled man ever elected to that office, and had enjoyed the greatest business experience. He was a scientist and executive, with none of the traditions of politician, orator or lawyer.

Early left an orphan, he was brought up by uncles in Iowa and Oregon and educated, largely through his own efforts, at Stanford University in California. Within a few years he was a successful mining engineer, accepting positions of increasing importance in Australia, China, Africa and other parts of the world. When the World War broke out in 1914 he was in England, and following his aid to American refugees, he became the leader in war relief work in devastated Belgium.

President Wilson named him United States Food Administrator when we entered the war. Later, he organized great food relief projects in Europe, and President Harding named him Secretary of Commerce.

By 1928 he was the world's best known citizen, and America's outstanding leader. He won the presidency from Governor Alfred E. Smith, of New York, the Democratic choice, in an election which saw the largest total vote ever recorded up to that time and a sharp breaking of party lines in many states.

President Hoover started White House Conferences on housing and child health and urged conservation of natural resources. In October 1929 the stock market crash began a depression, with world-wide effects. Hoover set up the Reconstruction Finance Corporation and Federal Home Loan Bank, and expanded the Farm Loan Bank, but conditions grew ever worse. Demanding change in national leadership, voters swept a Democrat, F.D. Roosevelt, into office in 1932.

FRANKLIN DELANO ROOSEVELT, *Thirty-second President*—March 4, 1933—April 12, 1945

BORN January 30, 1882, Hyde Park, N.Y. Of Dutch lineage. Son of James Roosevelt, capitalist and landholder, and Sara Delano. Educated at Harvard University and Columbia University Law School. An Episcopalian.

DIED April 12, 1945 of cerebral hemorrhage at Warm Springs, Ga. Buried in Hyde Park, N.Y.

MARRIED, in 1905, Anna Eleanor Roosevelt, a distant cousin. Six children.

Elections

1932.	Votes	
	Electoral: 531	Popular:
F.D. Roosevelt, D.	472	22,809,638
Herbert Hoover, R.	59	15,758,901
1936.	Electoral: 531	
F.D. Roosevelt, D.	523	27,752,869
Alfred M. Landon, R.	8	16,674,665
1940.	Electoral: 531	
F.D. Roosevelt, D.	449	27,307,819
Wendell Willkie, R.	82	22,321,018
1944.	Electoral: 531	
F.D. Roosevelt, D.	432	25,606,585
Thomas E. Dewey, R.	99	22,014,745

VICE PRESIDENTS; 1st and 2nd terms, John Nance Garner of Texas; 3rd term, Henry A. Wallace of Iowa; 4th term, Harry S. Truman of Missouri.

FRANKLIN DELANO ROOSEVELT entered public life in 1910 as a member of the New York Senate. He became Assistant Secretary of the Navy in 1913 under Woodrow Wilson, and in 1920 was Democratic nominee for Vice President, running unsuccessfully with James M. Cox of Ohio. In 1928 and 1930 he was elected Governor of New York. In November 1932, he was elected President by the largest vote, popular and electoral, ever recorded in a presidential election—and in 1936 by an even greater majority.

Entering his first term in a period of unemployment and depression, Roosevelt inaugurated the sweeping reforms which became known as the New Deal. He declared a bank holiday, sponsored legislation for the benefit of agriculture and labor, and set in motion a vast public works program.

Roosevelt was the first President to be inaugurated on January 20 (1941) under the 20th Amendment and the first to be elected for a third term. This term was marked by the entry of the United States into the ranks of the nations fighting the Axis powers in World War II. The President called for a new world order, based upon four freedoms (of speech, of religion, from want, from fear), and instituted a program for effective mobilization of the nation's military and economic resources. He participated in several important conferences abroad.

In 1944, Roosevelt was renominated for a fourth term; in November, he defeated his Republican opponent, Thomas E. Dewey, Governor of New York.

In February 1945, President Roosevelt conferred at Yalta in the Crimea with Winston Churchill and Stalin concerning the progress of the war and post-war settlements. This second meeting of the "Big Three" was one of the most important conferences in modern history.

HARRY S. TRUMAN, *Thirty-third President*—April 12, 1945—January 20, 1953

BORN May 8, 1884 in Lamar, Missouri, of English and Scotch-Irish ancestry. Son of John Anderson, a farmer, and Martha Ellen (Young) Truman. Attended public schools, Field Artillery School, Fort Sill, Oklahoma, and Kansas City School of Law. A farmer. A Baptist.

MARRIED June 28, 1919 Bess Wallace. One daughter, (Mary) Margaret.

Succeeded to the presidency of the United States upon the death of Franklin D. Roosevelt, April 12, 1945.

DIED December 26, 1972, aged 88, at his home in Independence, Mo. He is buried in Independence.

Election

1948.	Votes	
	Electoral: 531	Popular:
Harry S. Truman, D.	303	24,105,812
Thomas E. Dewey, R.	189	21,970,065
J. Strom Thurmond, S. Rts.	39	1,169,063
Henry A. Wallace, Prog.	0	1,157,172

VICE PRESIDENT: Alben W. Barkley of Kentucky.

WHEN Harry S. Truman became President after serving as Vice President only 82 days, he was known to the nation chiefly as a Senator (from 1934) and as the able chairman of the Senate committee set up in 1941 to investigate the national defense problem.

The war with Germany was near its end and the San Francisco Conference for Organization of the United Nations about to begin. On May 8, 1945, war ended in Europe. On July 17, Truman, Churchill, and Stalin met at Potsdam, Germany to begin the Berlin Conference. On July 26, Truman and Churchill issued a demand for unconditional surrender by Japan. On August 6, the United States dropped the world's first atomic bomb on Hiroshima. On the 8th, Russia declared war on Japan as of the next day. On the 9th, the second atomic bomb was dropped, on Nagasaki. On the 14th, Japan surrendered.

Truman's many postwar problems included labor and industrial unrest caused by the shift from war to peacetime economy, and a growing breach with the Soviet Union because of its aggressive tactics in seizing territory and power. In 1946, the Republicans swept the Congressional elections and gained control of both houses. Truman's election in 1948, with a Democratic Congress, was therefore a great political surprise.

On March 12, 1947, President Truman announced to Congress his doctrine of resistance to international aggression wherever it appeared, thus laying a foundation for the Marshall Plan for European recovery. When North Korean troops, spearheaded by Russian-built tanks, invaded the Republic of Korea on June 25, 1950, and the U.N. Security Council appealed to U.N. members for help in stopping hostilities, Truman on June 27 ordered "police action" by U.S. forces. The conflict grew into the Korean War (1950-1953).

DWIGHT D. EISENHOWER, *Thirty-fourth President*—January 20, 1953—January 20, 1961

BORN Denison, Texas, October 14, 1890, the third son of David Jacob and Ida Elizabeth Stover Eisenhower. Ancestors were German Mennonites who migrated to Switzerland, came to the United States in 1732 to escape religious persecution, and settled in Pennsylvania. Attended public schools in Abilene, Kansas, and graduated from United States Military Academy in 1915. Presbyterian.

MARRIED to Mamie Doud in Denver, Colorado, July 1, 1916. Two sons: Dwight Doud, who died as a child, and John Sheldon Doud Eisenhower.

DIED March 28, 1969, in Washington, D.C., of congestive heart failure, aged 78. Buried at Abilene, Kansas.

Elections

1952.	Votes	
	Electoral: 531	Popular:
Dwight D. Eisenhower, R.	442	33,936,234
Adlai E. Stevenson, D.	89	27,314,992
1956.	Electoral: 531	
Dwight D. Eisenhower, R.	457	35,590,472
Adlai E. Stevenson, D.	73	26,022,752
Walter B. Jones, Alabama	1	——

VICE PRESIDENT: Richard Milhous Nixon of California.

In 1952 the nation chose as its President General Dwight D. Eisenhower, a man known throughout the world for his distinguished military career. He had been called to Washington five days after Pearl Harbor to assume staff duties; on June 25, 1942, he had become Supreme Commander of Allied Expeditionary Forces, responsible for planning and carrying out the gigantic Normandy invasion. In postwar years, General Eisenhower was Army Chief of Staff, President of Columbia University, and (after recall to military duty by President Truman) Supreme Commander in Europe of NATO forces.

In 1952, he yielded to demands to run for President on the Republican ticket. On May 31 he retired from active military service, and on July 18, resigned from the Army. He won a sweeping victory over Adlai E. Stevenson in 1952; in 1956, with Stevenson again his Democratic opponent, he was re-elected by an even greater popular and electoral vote than in 1952.

As President, Eisenhower stressed the U.S. mission of leadership in world affairs. Fighting was stopped in Korea, NATO was strengthened, and the Southeast Asia Treaty Organization formed. Eisenhower met with heads of other nations and visited foreign countries in his efforts to help solve the problems of ever-increasing international tensions. Rulers and political leaders from all parts of the world visited Washington.

Notable events early in his administration were the creation in 1953 of the Department of Health, Education, and Welfare, in 1954, the successful test of the first hydrogen bomb, and in 1954, the agreement for the St. Lawrence Seaway. In the first year of his second term the world's "Age of Space" began, on October 4, 1957, with the launching by the Soviet Union of the first man-made satellite. Alaska and Hawaii became the Union's 49th and 50th states in 1959, the first new states since 1912.

JOHN F. KENNEDY, *Thirty-fifth President*—January 20, 1961-November 22, 1963

BORN May 29, 1917, in Brookline, Mass., second son of Joseph P. and Rose (Fitzgerald) Kennedy. His father, financier and politician, was U.S. Ambassador to Great Britain, 1937-1941. His maternal grandfather, John F. Fitzgerald, "Honey Fitz", was a U.S. Representative and Mayor of Boston—Irish descent, Roman Catholic.

DIED November 22, 1963, aged 46. Shot by an assassin at Dallas, Texas, while in a motorcade. Death came within minutes. Buried at Arlington National Cemetery, Arlington, Va.

MARRIED Sept. 12, 1953, Jacqueline Lee Bouvier. Children: Caroline, born Nov. 27, 1957; John Fitzgerald, Jr., born Nov. 25, 1960.

Election

1960.	Votes	
	Electoral: 537	Popular:
John F. Kennedy, D.	303	34,221,531
Richard M. Nixon, R.	219	34,108,474
Harry F. Byrd, D., Va.	15	——
Others	—	502,773

VICE PRESIDENT: Lyndon B. Johnson of Texas.

JOHN FITZGERALD KENNEDY was the youngest man, and the first Roman Catholic, ever elected to the presidency. He was also the first to have carried his campaign into voters' homes by means of television debates with his opponent.

Kennedy's education was obtained at the London(England) School of Economics, 1935-36, at Harvard (B.S., cum laude, 1940), and at Stanford University. In September 1941 he enlisted in the U.S. Navy, commanded a PT-boat in the South Pacific 1941-45, and for heroic action when his boat was rammed and sunk, was awarded the Navy and Marine Corps Medal. In March 1945 he was retired from active duty.

Less than three months after Kennedy became President, the first of two Cuban crises occurred—an unsuccessful invasion by Cuban exiles of their homeland. In October 1962 it was revealed that the Soviet Union had established missile bases in Cuba. Kennedy ordered a blockade of the island and demanded that Russia remove its missiles and reduce military forces there. Within several weeks the Soviets had complied and world-wide tension eased.

In February 1962, Lt. Col. John H. Glenn, Jr. became the first American to orbit the earth. Steel prices were increased in 1962 but were cut back again after the President denounced the action and asked steel manufacturers to hold the price line. The year 1963 was one of major Negro civil rights demonstrations in the United States. A broad civil rights program was urged by President Kennedy.

During the Kennedy administration, the Peace Corps was established, and an international nuclear test ban treaty was signed; also, acts for trade expansion, aid to depressed areas, and an increase in the minimum wage were signed.

LYNDON BAINES JOHNSON, *Thirty-sixth President*—November 22, 1963—January 20, 1969

BORN August 27, 1908, near Stonewall, Texas, eldest son of Samuel Ealy and Rebekah Baines Johnson. Ancestors were primarily English, although some came from Ireland, Germany, Scotland, and France. Samuel Ealy Johnson, school teacher and farmer, was a member of the Texas legislature, and Rebekah Baines' grandfather, George Washington Baines, Sr., was a president of Baylor University. Lyndon attended Blanco County public schools and was graduated from Southwest Texas State Teachers College in 1930.

MARRIED Claudia Alta (Lady Bird) Taylor on November 17, 1934. Two daughters: Lynda Bird, born March 19, 1944: Lucy Baines, born July 2, 1947.

DIED January 22, 1973 of a heart attack, aged 64. He is buried on his ranch near the Pedernales River.

1964.	Election Votes	
	Electoral: 538	Popular:
Lyndon B. Johnson, D.	486	43,121,085
Barry Goldwater, R.	52	27,145,161

VICE PRESIDENT: Hubert H. Humphrey of Minnesota.

LYNDON BAINES JOHNSON, one of the most politically experienced men to hold the office of President, had about 23 years as a Member of Congress and almost three years as Vice President.

Johnson began as a public school teacher in Houston, Texas. From 1931-35 he was secretary to Representative Kleberg of Texas, and was then appointed Texas State Director of the National Youth Administration by President Roosevelt. In 1937 he resigned to run for Congress and won a special election. He was reelected in 1938 and for the four succeeding terms.

On December 10, 1941, Johnson enlisted in the U.S. Navy and was commissioned lieutenant commander. Stationed in New Zealand and Australia, he participated as an observer on several bomber missions in the South Pacific. He was awarded the Silver Star before returning to the House in mid-1942 after a ruling that national legislators might not serve in the armed forces.

Lyndon Johnson was elected to the U.S. Senate in 1948 and reelected in 1954. He was minority leader in the 83rd Congress, and majority leader in the 84th to 86th Congresses. Johnson made a bid for the Democratic Presidential nomination in 1960, losing to John Kennedy, but was chosen as the Party's nominee for Vice President. As Vice President, he served as chairman of the Committee on Government Contracts, and headed the National Aeronautics and Space Council and the President's Committee on Equal Employment Opportunities.

Lyndon Johnson was elected to his first full term by a large majority in 1964.

President Johnson was responsible for an $11.5 billion tax cut and, in 1968, a 10 per cent income tax surcharge. He named the first Negro to the Supreme Court and fought civil rights inequities and poverty. He mustered all his resources in an attempt to end the war in Vietnam.

RICHARD MILHOUS NIXON, *Thirty-Seventh President*–Jan.20, 1969—Aug 9, 1974

BORN January 9, 1913, in Yorba Linda, California, second of five sons of Francis Anthony and Hannah Milhous Nixon. Welsh-Irish. Quaker. Francis Anthony Nixon ran a citrus farm in Yorba Linda and, later, a combination grocery store and gasoline station in Whittier. Richard Nixon was graduated from Whittier College in 1934 and Duke University Law School in 1937, and he was president of both student bodies. Quaker.

MARRIED Thelma Catherine Patricia Ryan on June 21, 1940. Two daughters: Patricia (Tricia), born February 21, 1946, and Julie, born July 5, 1948.

1968.	Election Votes	
	Electoral: 538	Popular:
Richard M. Nixon, R.	301	31,770,237
Hubert H. Humphrey, D.	191	31,270,533
George C. Wallace, Ind.	46	9,906,141
1974.		
Richard M. Nixon, R.	521	47,165,234
George S. McGovern, D.	17	29,168,110

VICE PRESIDENTS: Spiro T. Agnew of Maryland and Gerald Rudolph Ford of Michigan.

RICHARD M. NIXON, one of the most governmentally-experienced men ever elected President of the U.S., also made one of the greatest political comebacks. Defeated for the Presidency in 1960 and for the Governorship of California in 1962, he returned to private law practice in New York.

Dedicated work for Republican candidates in subsequent elections aided immensely in his successful bid for the 1968 nomination.

In 1946, at age 33, Lt. Cmdr. Nixon was engaged in legal business for the Navy when he was suggested as a candidate for Congress from California. In Congress, he helped draft and fought for passage of the Taft-Harley Act, which provides for an 80-day delay of strikes that threaten the national interest.

Congressman Nixon led an investigation which led to conviction of Alger Hiss for lying under oath when he denied having committed espionage.

An active Vice President, he visited 56 foreign countries including Latin America in 1958 and the Soviet Union in 1959 where he had a famous confrontation with Premier Khrushchev at an American exhibit in Moscow. He also filled the vacuum of the President's office on three occasions when President Eisenhower was severely ill.

He was nominated by acclamation as the Republican nominee for President in 1960. During the campaign, he visited all 50 states and carried 26 of them in the election, although losing to John F. Kennedy by the closest popular vote margin in presidential election history.

President Nixon opened up relations with Mainland China and improved relations with the Soviet Union. He ended U.S. involvement in the Vietnam War, bringing home half a million troops and prisoners of war.

He won 49 of the 50 states in his 1972 reelection. Nevertheless, he resigned in 1974 because of the Watergate affair.

GERALD RUDOLPH FORD, Thirty-eighth President—August 9, 1974—January 20, 1977

BORN July 14, 1913, in Omaha, Neb., of Leslie and Dorothy Gardner King.

He received a BA degree from Michigan University in 1935, and a Law degree from Yale in 1941. He has been admitted to practice before the U.S. Supreme Court. He was a three-varsity letter man at Michigan and played on national championship football teams in 1932-3. Episcopalian.

MARRIED Elizabeth Bloomer on Oct. 15, 1948. Children: Michael, born March 15, 1950; John, born March 16, 1952; Steven, born, May 19, 1956; Susan, born July 6, 1957.

VICE PRESIDENT: Nelson A. Rockefeller of New York.

Gerald Rudolph Ford is the only President to fill the office without being voted on in a national election. He was appointed Vice President in 1973 and became President on August 9, 1974 upon the resignation of President Nixon.

Most of Ford's political career had been spent in the U.S. House of Representatives. He served as Representative from Michigan's Fifth Congressional District from 1949 until he resigned in 1973 to become the Vice President. Ford was elected 13 times to the House, always with winning percentages of 60 or more.

Ford had said his ambition was to become Speaker of the House, difficult for any Republican in recent decades, since that party has seldom controlled the House. However, he was named by House Republicans to become the Minority Leader at the opening of the 89th Congress in January 1965. Two years earlier, he had been chosen as chairman of the Republican Conference of the House, and he served more than nine years on the House Republican Committee.

In his 25-year House career, Ford had an attendance record of better than 90 per cent.

In almost 2 1/2 years as President, Ford vetoed a number of spending bills, saving some $13 billion in costs to the federal government.

The rate of inflation during his period in the White House was halved and unemployment lessened.

He won the Republican nomination for President in a close race with former California Gov. Ronald Reagan. In the general election, he carried 27 states but lost to Jimmy Carter by one of the closest electoral votes in presidential voting history.

JAMES EARL CARTER, Jr. Thirty-ninth President—January 20, 1977—January 20, 1981

BORN October 1, 1924 in Plains, Ga., son of James Earl and Lillian Gordy Carter.

He was graduated from the U.S. Naval Academy in 1947 and did graduate work in nuclear physics at Union College. He served in the Navy from 1947-53, rising to the rank of lieutenant. A Baptist.

MARRIED Rosalynn Smith on July 7, 1946. Three sons: John William (Jack), born in 1947; James Earl III (Chip), born in 1950; Donnel Jeffrey, born in 1952. Daughter Amy Lynn was born in 1967.

1976.	**Election Votes**	
	Electoral: 538	Popular:
James E. Carter, D.	297	40,291,626
Gerald R. Ford, R.	241	38,563,089

VICE PRESIDENT: Walter F. Mondale of Minnesota.

James Earl Carter, a small town peanut farmer, was the first Georgian to win the presidency. Carter won the Democratic nomination in 1976 over a dozen other contenders, well known figures who might have been expected to outperform him. But Carter and his family worked hard for several prior years, and as national chairman for the 1974 Democratic congressional campaign he traveled extensively and built his base.

Carter was a Georgia state senator from 1962-66 and governor from 1971-74. State law prohibited his serving a second term.

Advocating administrative streamlining, Carter indicated he would serve as a populist President.

However, the very things he emphasized in debates with President Gerald Ford - inflation, unemployment, taxes - contributed substantially to his undoing in his second bid for the office. Inflation worsened considerably during the Carter years, and unemployment remained relatively high. He also failed in his prediction of balancing the federal budget.

Carter's "human rights" policy was criticized by Republicans and some Democrats as contributing to America's weakness around the world. Some said it helped cause the ouster of the Shah of Iran. For 14 months, Carter had the deep problem of trying to win release of the more than 50 staff members of the U.S. embassy in Iran who were captured and held prisoner.

Carter worked hard to bring peace to the Middle East and he was involved in a partial settlement between Egypt and Israel.

However, he was overwhelmingly defeated by Republican Ronald W. Reagan in the 1980 presidential election, winning only six states in his reelection bid.

RONALD WILSON REAGAN, *Fortieth President*—January 20, 1981—January 20, 1989

BORN February 6, 1911, in Tampico, Ill., older son of John and Nelle Wilson Reagan.

He was graduated from Eureka College in 1932 with a degree in economics and sociology. He served in the Army Air Corps from April 1942 to December 1945, rising to the rank of captain. A member of the Christian Church.

MARRIED Jane Wyman on Jan. 25, 1940; divorced in 1948. Married Nancy Davis on March 4, 1952. Children are Maureen, born in 1941; Michael, born in 1945; Patricia, born in 1952, and Ronald, born in 1958.

1980.	Election Votes	
	Electoral: 538	Popular:
Ronald W. Reagan, R.	489	42,797,153
James E. Carter, D.	49	34,434,100
John B. Anderson, Ind.		5,533,927

VICE PRESIDENT: George H. Bush of Texas

Election Results— 1984/Second Term

	Electoral Vote	Popular Vote
Ronald W. Reagan, R.	525	54,451,521
Walter F. Mondale, D.	13	37,565,334

Ronald Wilson Reagan won the presidency by carrying 44 of the 50 states. With his big victory came the first Republican control of a house of Congress—the Senate—since the Eisenhower years. In 1984, he easily won his second term in a landslide victory.

Reagan had been president of his union, the Screen Actors Guild, for six terms and he was twice elected president of the Motion Picture Industry Council. His earlier career included stints as sports broadcaster and editor, and a film career that includes 53 feature-length motion pictures. He was also a television actor and series host in the 1950s and '60s, and he was a featured General Electric Co. speaker.

He began his quest for public office after he had made a very successful speech on behalf of Republican presidential nominee Barry M. Goldwater in 1964. Reagan was elected governor of California in 1966 by a million votes, and he was reelected by a large majority in 1970. Reagan sought the Republican presidential nomination in 1976, losing by only a handful of delegates, to President Gerald Ford. In the years afterward, he remained in the public eye by writing a syndicated newspaper column and by broadcasting commentary five times weekly over hundreds of radio stations.

Reagan's theme had been a conservative form of government. He had consistently called for reducing the size of government and of balancing the federal budget. He was an ardent anti-communist and early in his administration criticized the Soviet Union for that nation's interference in the affairs of other countries.

Reagan called for substantial cuts in the budget and in federal programs. He urged more deregulation and less government control over the affairs of business, and he proposed an individual tax cut that would amount to 30 percent in three years.

Reagan was unusual in that he appealed to both Republicans and Democrats and made a point of working closely with the Democrats in Congress. Even though he won the presidency by a substantial margin, he improved his popularity after taking office.

On March 30, 1981, President Reagan was shot and wounded in an assassination attempt in Washington, D.C. He never ceased his duties while recovering.

GEORGE HERBERT WALKER BUSH, *Forty-first President*—January 20, 1989—January 20, 1993

BORN June 12, 1924, in Milton, Massachusetts to Prescott Sheldon Bush and Dorothy Walker Bush.

He graduated from Yale University, Phi Beta Kappa, in 1948 with a degree in economics.

During World War II, he served as a Navy pilot, seeing action in the Pacific.

MARRIED Barbara Pierce on January 6, 1945. Children are George Walker, John Ellis, Neil Mallon, Marvin Pierce, and Dorothy Walker.

1988	**Election Votes**	
	Electoral: 538	Popular:
George H.W. Bush, R.	426	47,946,422
Michael Dukakis, D.	112	41,016,429

VICE PRESIDENT: J. Danforth Quayle of Indiana

George Herbert Walker Bush is a President who had served his country in more Federal capacities than his predecessors.

As World War II raged on, George Bush became the youngest pilot in the U.S. Navy, flying torpedo bombers in the Pacific. He saw combat, having his plane shot down at sea. He was awarded the Distinguished Flying Cross and three air medals.

After graduating from Yale University, he made Texas his home, working in the oil and drilling business.

His father, Prescott Bush, Senator from Connecticut, set the tone for George Bush's life. Bush started in public service in 1966, being elected to the House of Representative. In 1971, he was appointed by President Nixon as our ambassador to the United Nations. He was chairman of the Republican National Committee in 1973.

President Ford chose Bush for two delicate positions. The first was in 1974, to become Chief of the U.S. Liaison Office in the People's Republic of China, the second was as Director of the Central Intelligence Agency in 1976.

During the eight successful years of the Reagan presidency, George Bush served as Vice-President. On July 13, 1985, Bush was named acting President for several hours under the 25th amendment while Reagan was undergoing surgery.

George Bush's overwhelming election to the Presidency was a vote of confidence in a life-long successful federal career.

During 1991, President Bush committed 500,000 U.S. troops, along with armies from allied nations, to the Persian Gulf in an effort to free an invaded Kuwait.

The ensuing war with the invader, Iraq, was led by the largest allied air campaign ever conducted.

The ground assault, which lasted 100 hours with minimal casualties, was an overwhelming victory for the United States, the allies and Kuwait.

At the end of his term the United States could look back on the end of the Cold War, the demise of the Soviet Union, and the reunification of the two Germanys.

WILLIAM JEFFERSON CLINTON, *Forty-Second President*—January 20, 1993

BORN August 19, 1946 in Hope, Arkansas to William Jefferson Blyth, III and Virginia Cassidy Blyth. He received a Bachelor's degree from Georgetown University and then spent two years at Oxford University as a Rhodes Scholar. He later earned a law degree from Yale in 1973.

MARRIED Hillary Rodham in 1975. They have one child, Chelsea, born in 1980.

1992	Election Vote	
	Electoral: 538	Popular
Bill Clinton, D.	370	43,728,375
George H.W. Bush, R.	168	38,167,416
H. Ross Perot, Ind.	0	19,237,247

VICE PRESIDENT: Albert Gore, Jr. of Tennessee

From a handshake with the then President, John F. Kennedy, on the White House lawn in 1963 to the Presidential Inauguration of 1993, William (Bill) Jefferson Clinton had pursued and realized a lifelong dream. He became the 42nd President of the United States.

The President was born William Jefferson Blyth, IV, two months after his father, William Jefferson Blyth, III, died in a traffic accident. His mother married and divorced Roger Clinton, Jr. She then married Jeff Dwire, and later Richard Kelley.

Bill Clinton became President after serving five terms as the Democratic Governor of Arkansas and one term as its attorney general.

As Governor of Arkansas, he worked with its Legislature to enact major education, health, and environmental packages, a highway program, tougher child abuse and domestic abuse laws, tax reforms, and welfare programs.

The race for President saw the young Arkansas Governor running against President Bush, with twelve years of Republican domination of the office and Independent H. Ross Perot, a successful businessman from Texas. Clinton beat his opponents by focusing on the then current economic conditions, the need for change, and Clinton as a "new kind of Democrat" for whom change did not mean a return to "tax and spend" policies associated in the past with Democrats.

Wives and Families of the Presidents

Martha Washington

Abigail Adams

GEORGE WASHINGTON'S ADMINISTRATION

Martha Washington (1731-1802) was the daughter of Col. John Dandridge, a planter of New Kent County, Va., and the widow of Daniel Park Custis, also a wealthy planter, when she married Washington (1759). She had four children, two living at the time of her second marriage. The Washingtons had no children.

When Washington became President she went with him to New York, where they took a house, and later to Philadelphia, where she entertained in formal style throughout his administration. Guests found the presidential table abundant, the hospitality sincere but quite formal. At Mt. Vernon the Washingtons kept many servants and lived very well.

JOHN ADAMS' ADMINSTRATION

Abigail Adams (1744-1818) was the daughter of a Congregationalist minister, the Rev. William Smith, and came from a long line of Puritans. She was a capable housewife and manager, and during her husband's long service abroad she maintained the farm at Quincy, reared and educated the children, and was sometimes hard pressed for funds, since John's salary was meagre, continental money was of small value, and crops hard to raise and harder to sell. She made one trip to England.

Adams was inaugurated in Philadelphia, but soon thereafter the capital moved to the new city of Washington, where Abigail became the mistress of the President's House, later to be called the White House. It was incomplete, and she used the audience rooms for clothes drying and had to employ many other makeshifts. She entertained considerably and in formal fashion, sharing her husband's belief that the presidency should carry some of the dignity of the courts of Europe.

Dolley Madison

Elizabeth Monroe

Jefferson's Administration

Martha Wayles Skelton Jefferson (1748-1782) the tall, brown-eyed, vivacious daughter of John Wayles, a wealthy lawyer of Charles City County, Va., married Bathurst Skelton, who died before she was twenty. She became the bride of Thomas Jefferson in 1772. They had six children, two of whom, both girls, lived to maturity. Martha died nineteen years before her husband became President, and he never married again. The eldest daughter, Martha, wife of Thomas Randolph, kept house for her father for many years.

At the White House, Jefferson lived a quiet existence, did away with the formal levees, and held two public receptions a year.

Madison's Administration

The handsome, vivacious Dolley Madison (1768-1849) was the daughter of John Payne of North Carolina. Her mother, Mary Coles, was a cousin of Patrick Henry. She was reared a Quaker, and at 19 married John Todd, a Quaker lawyer from Philadelphia, who died in the yellow fever epidemic in 1793. They had two sons. In Philadelphia, where the government was located, the statesmen of the time met and admired the fair widow Todd, and she refused many a fine offer, only to wed the serious, quiet, rotund Madison. She and Madison had no children.

Martha Jefferson Randolph

Dolley supplied all the social graces which the serious James lacked, and when he became Secretary of State under Jefferson, she became the social leader in Washington. Her reign continued through her husband's two terms and long thereafter, and years later as an old woman she was feted and toasted when she came to the capital.

Louisa Catherine Adams

Rachel Jackson

MONROE'S ADMINISTRATION

Elizabeth Monroe (1768-1830) was born in New York City, the daughter of Capt. Lawrence Kortright of the British Army. One sister married M. Heyliger, Grand Chamberlain to the King of Denmark. Another married Nicholas Gouverneur of New York. The Monroes had two daughters, one of whom married George Hay of Virginia. The other married, at the White House, her cousin, Samuel L. Gouverneur of New York.

Mrs. Monroe had traveled in Europe with her husband, was an accomplished hostess, and did the honors at the White House throughout his two terms in office.

JOHN QUINCY ADAMS' ADMINISTRATION

Louisa Catherine Adams (1775-1852) was the daughter of Joshua Johnson of Maryland, but was born in London, where her father was fiscal agent for the colonies and the new government for many years. Adams met and married her in London, and they lived abroad for many years while he was minister in London, Berlin, and St. Petersburg.

At the White House, the hospitality of the Adams regime became famous. Louisa Adams gave notable receptions and levees. In 1828, at the White House, the Adams' second son, John, was married to his cousin, Mary Catherine Hellen.

Charles Francis Adams, the third son, was active in politics, and became Free Soil candidate for the Vice President in 1848. Lincoln made him Minister to England in 1861.

JACKSON'S ADMINISTRATION

Rachel Donelson Robards Jackson (1767-1828) did not live to see her husband in the White House, but she was a striking figure in his earlier career. The daughter of Col. John Donelson

Letitia C. Tyler

Sarah C. Polk

of Virginia, she went with her father as a girl to frontier Tennessee. Her first husband, Capt. Lewis Robards, applied to the Virginia legislature in 1790 for a divorce, and was granted the right to sue for one. Believing this a grant of divorce, she married General Jackson at Natchez in 1791. Later, she learned the divorce proceedings had not been completed. When the decree was granted, the Jacksons were remarried, on Jan. 17, 1794.

She was a valued helpmate to her fiery soldier husband. They had no children, but adopted a son of her sister, who was named Andrew Jackson, Jr., and inherited the President's estates. Rachel died the year of Jackson's election to the presidency. Her niece, Emily, whose husband and cousin, Maj. A. J. Donelson, was Jackson's private secretary, did the honors at the White House.

Van Buren's Administration

Hannah Hoes Van Buren (1783-1819) was a distant cousin of Van Buren's mother, Mary Hoes, and was a classmate of Van Buren at school in Kinderhook, New York. She died before her husband became President. Of their sons, Abraham was a West Point graduate, served on the Western frontier, was secretary to his father and later an officer in the Mexican War. John was once Attorney General of New York, and died at sea. Abraham's wife, Angelica Singleton of South Carolina, was a cousin of Dolley Madison. She was mistress of the White House during her father-in-law's term.

Angelica Van Buren

Harrison and Tyler Administrations

Anna Symmes Harrison (1775-1864) was the daughter of Col. John Cleves Symmes, a delegate to the Continental Congress, a Revolutionary soldier and later Supreme Court judge in New Jersey. Mrs. Harrison was an invalid at the time of her husband's election, and did not come to the White House, but she outlived him by a quarter of a century. Mrs. Jane

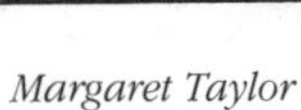

Margaret Taylor

Abigail P. Fillmore

Irwin Harrison, widow of W. H. Harrison, Jr., was at the White House during the brief weeks before President Harrison died.

The first Mrs. Tyler, Letitia Christian (1790-1842) was the daughter of a Virginia planter, Robert Christian of New Kent County. She was an invalid when Tyler took office, and died at the White House. Her son Robert married Priscilla, daughter of T. A. Cooper, the tragedian, and she did the honors at the White House prior to Tyler's second marriage.

Julia Gardiner (1820-1889) was born on Gardiner's Island, her family manor, near Easthampton, New York. She was married to President Tyler in New York on June 26, 1844. One of their sons, Lyon Gardiner Tyler, became president of William and Mary College.

Polk's Administration

Sarah Childress Polk (1803-1891) was the daughter of Capt. Joel Childress, a wealthy planter near Murfreesboro, Tennessee. She was a decided beauty, of the Spanish type, and educated at a Moravian school. She was strict about temperance observance, and abolished wine and dancing at White House receptions. The Polks had no children. After her husband's death she adopted a niece.

Taylor and Fillmore Administrations

Margaret Smith Taylor (1788-1852) was the daughter of Walter Smith, a planter of Calvert County, Maryland. She was of delicate health and her daughter Elizabeth (Betty), who married Maj. W. W. S. Bliss, did the honors at the White House. Another daughter, Sarah, married Jefferson Davis, who became President of the Confederacy. The Taylor's son, Richard, served under Stonewall Jackson.

Abigail Powers Fillmore (1798-1853) was the daughter of the Rev. Lemuel Powers, a Baptist

Mary Todd Lincoln

Eliza M. Johnson

preacher in Saratoga County, N.Y. She was a school teacher, both before and after her marriage, in 1826. When Fillmore succeeded to the presidency she was an invalid, and her daughter, Abigail, presided at White House functions. Mrs. Fillmore died a few weeks after the close of her husband's administration.

Pierce's Administration

Jane Appleton Pierce (1806-1863) was the daughter of the Rev. Jesse Appleton, president of Bowdoin College, where Franklin Pierce met her. They had three sons, but none lived to manhood. Two died, and a third was killed in a railroad accident at the age of 13, two months before his father became President. Mrs. Pierce was a gracious and well-loved hostess in the White House.

Buchanan's Administration

James Buchanan was the bachelor President and the First Lady during his administration was his niece, Harriet Lane, who later married Henry Elliot Johnston, of Baltimore. Miss Lane, as the White House hostess, had the distinction of entertaining the Prince of Wales, who became King Edward VII.

Jane Appleton Pierce

Lincoln's Administration

Mary Todd Lincoln (1818-1882) was the daughter of Robert Todd, a pioneer settler from Lexington, Kentucky. At the White House Mrs. Lincoln had little occasion for social distinction, owing to the war, and devoted her time to war work and to the care of her family.

Harriet Lane

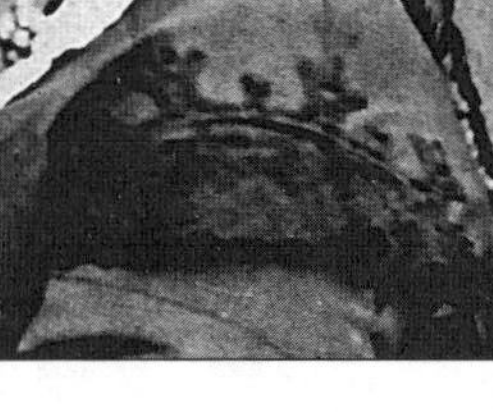

Julia Dent Grant

Lucy Webb Hayes

Andrew Johnson's Administration

Eliza McCardle Johnson (1810-1876) was the only daughter of a widowed mother, and was teaching school in a mountain village in Tennessee when Johnson met and married her. She helped educate her husband, who had never been a day at school. Their daughter Martha was sent to school at Georgetown, and was often a guest at the White House in Polk's time. She married Judge D. T. Patterson, and was hostess at the White House for her father, since Mrs. Johnson was in poor health.

Grant's Administration

Julia Dent Grant (1826-1902) was the daughter of Judge Frederick Dent of St. Louis, and a social favorite in that city when Grant as a young officer met and won her. Her social regime at the White House was climaxed by the wedding of their daughter, Nellie, to Capt. Algernon Sartoris of London. Two sons of the President achieved distinction as soldiers, Frederick Dent Grant being a general in the Spanish-American War. Mrs. Grant was one of the famous hostesses of the White House.

Hayes' Administration

Lucy Webb Hayes (1831-1889) was the daughter of Dr. James Webb of Chillicothe, Ohio. She was a college graduate and an ardent prohibitionist, never allowing wine to be served at the White House. Several of the large family of children were youngsters during the Hayes administration, and the family life at the mansion is recorded as having been delightful.

Lucretia Garfield

Frances Folsom Cleveland

Garfield and Arthur Administrations

Lucretia Rudolph Garfield (1832-1918) was the daughter of Zebulon Rudolph, a farmer from Garrettsville, Ohio. She and Garfield were schoolmates. Of their sons, Harry A. became president of Williams College, and James R. was Secretary of Interior under Theodore Roosevelt.

Ellen Herndon Arthur (1837-1880) was the daughter of Commander William Lewis Herndon of Fredericksburg, Va. Mrs. Arthur died before her husband became President. Arthur's sister, Mary, wife of John E. McElroy of Albany, presided at the White House during his term.

Cleveland's Administration

Frances Folsom Cleveland (1864-1947) was a White House bride of a President. Her father was Oscar Folsom, a law partner of Cleveland's in Buffalo. Prior to their marriage, the President's sister, Rose Elizabeth Cleveland, was mistress at the White House. The bride, youngest wife of a President, was First Lady during the last part of Cleveland's first term and all of his second. One of their daughters was born at the White House. A son, Richard, served in the Marine Corps in World War I. Five years after the death of Cleveland, his widow married (1913) Thomas J. Preston, Jr., a professor at Princeton University.

Mary McElroy

Caroline S. Harrison

Ida S. McKinley

Harrison's Administration

Carolina Scott Harrison (1832-1892) was the daughter of Prof. John W. Scott of Miami University, Ohio. She died at the White House near the end of her husband's term. She was the first President-General of the Daughters of the American Revolution. She was a musician and painter. Their son, Russell B., was a mining engineer and journalist. Their daughter, Mary, married James R. Mc Kee of Indianapolis.
The second Mrs. Harrison was a niece of the first. She was Mary Scott Lord Dimmick (1858-1948), the widow of Walter E. Dimmick, a lawyer from New York. She married Harrison in New York in 1896. Their daughter, Elizabeth, married James Blaine Walker, Jr.

McKinley's Administration

Ida Saxton McKinley (1847-1907) was the daughter of James A. Saxton, a banker from Canton, Ohio. She had been educated at home and abroad and was cashier at her father's bank at the time of her marriage. Her two daughters died in childhood, and she was an invalid for years, but presided at the White House and accompanied her husband everywhere. She was with him in Buffalo when he was assassinated.

Theodore Roosevelt's Administration

The first Mrs. Roosevelt, Alice Lee (1861-1884), daughter of George Cabot Lee of Boston, died two days after the birth of a daughter, Alice Lee Roosevelt. She was married at the White House in 1906 to Nicholas Longworth of Ohio, later Speaker of the House of Representatives.

Edith K. Roosevelt

Helen H. Taft

The second Mrs. Roosevelt was Edith Kermit Carow (1861-1948), daughter of Charles Carow of New York. They were married in London in 1886, and had four sons and one daughter. Mrs. Roosevelt was a charming mistress of the Executive Mansion and the leader of the social life of the capital. Her daughter, Ethel, married Richard Derby of New York. The four sons, Theodore, Kermit, Archie and Quentin, served in World War I; Quentin, an aviator, was killed in action. His three brothers served in World War II, as well. Theodore, Jr., a brigadier general, died in Normandy in 1944; Kermit, a major, died on active duty in Alaska in 1943. Archibald, a lieutenant colonel, was retired from active service in 1945.

Taft's Administration

Helen Herron Taft (1861-1943) was the daughter of Judge John W. Herron of Cincinnati, who was a law partner of President Hayes. Mrs. Taft was a musician. She was ill during part of her husband's term, and her sister, Mrs. Louis More, presided at official entertainments. Mrs. Taft's White House teas became famous.

Her daughter, Helen Herron Taft, married Prof. Frederick J. Manning of Yale; she became a successful educator. The Taft sons became lawyers. Charles P. Taft, in 1946, became the first layman president of the Federal Council of Churches of Christ in America. Robert A. Taft served in the Ohio legislature and was a prominent member in the United States Senate from 1939 until his death in 1953.

Ellen Axson Wilson

Edith Bolling Galt Wilson

Wilson's Administration

The first Mrs. Wilson was Ellen Louise Axson (1860-1914), daughter of the Rev. S. E. Axson and sister of Prof. Stockton Axson of Princeton. She was assisted as hostess at the White House by her three daughters, Eleanor, Jessie and Margaret. Eleanor married during her father's presidency, William G. McAdoo, Secretary of the Treasury, while Jessie became the bride of Francis B. Sayre, an educator. Mrs. Wilson died during her husband's first term.

The second Mrs. Wilson was Edith Bolling Galt (1872-1961) of Virginia, widow of Norman Galt, a jeweler, from Washington. She married the President in 1915, and was with him in Europe during the peace conference following the World War; she nursed him during his illness at the White House and subsequently until his death.

Harding's Administration

Florence Kling Harding (1860-1924) was the daughter of Amos Kling, a Marion, Ohio, merchant and banker. Her first husband was Henry DeWolfe, and they had one son. A divorce decree restored her maiden name. DeWolfe later died. The Hardings were married in 1891, and she helped her husband develop a small newspaper, the Marion Star, into a highly successful property. Mrs. Harding entered into the social life of the capital with enthusiastic energy, but was taken seriously ill. She recovered to some extent and was with her husband on the trip to Alaska and the West, when he died. She survived him a little more than a year.

Florence Kling Harding

Grace G. Coolidge

Coolidge's Administration

Grace Goodhue Coolidge (1879-1957) was the daughter of Capt. Andrew I. Goodhue and Lemira Barrett of Burlington, Vermont. She graduated from the University of Vermont and was a teacher at Clarke Institute for the Deaf, Northhampton, Mass., when she married Mr. Coolidge. Of the two sons, Calvin, born in 1908, died in Washington, July 7, 1924, of an infection of the foot, developing from a slight blister and John, born in 1906, married Florence Trumbull, daughter of Gov. John H. Trumbull of Connecticut.

Grace Coolidge endeared herself to the American people by her untiring courtesy, modesty, and example of the admired qualities of American womanhood. The social duties of the executive mansion were carried on with dignity and charm, and the White House breakfasts, at which many leaders in public affairs were guests, formed a feature of the official life of the capital which became famous.

Hoover's Administration

Lou Henry Hoover (1875-1944), daughter of Charles D. Henry, a banker of Waterloo, Iowa, moved with her family to California at an early age. At Stanford University she met her future husband, and they were married as soon as she had graduated from college. Mrs. Hoover lived with her family in many lands where her husband's work took him. She was a lover of the outdoors, a capable geologist, translated Latin scientific works, and was a charming hostess.

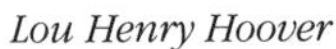

Lou Henry Hoover

Anna Eleanor Roosevelt

Mrs. Hoover was president of the Girl Scouts for a year and was its Honorary President. She aided in the many great relief projects headed by her husband at home and abroad.

During Mr. Hoover's eight years as Secretary of Commerce under Harding and Coolidge, the Hoover home in Washington was a center of friendly social atmosphere. Mrs. Hoover was an eminently capable Mistress of the White House-modest, gracious, and much admired.

Herbert Hoover, Jr., born in 1903, became a consulting engineer, and was Under Secretary of State from 1951-1956. Allen Henry Hoover, born in 1907, became a director of mining corporations.

Franklin D. Roosevelt's Administration

Anna Eleanor Roosevelt (1884-1962), was the daughter of Elliott and Anna (Hall) Roosevelt, and a distant cousin of her husband, the President. Born in New York City, she was educated at private schools and exhibited a continuing interest in educational work. Always keenly interested in political affairs, her equipment fitted her admirably for the exacting position of Mistress of the White House.

As wife of the President, she devoted herself to a career of social reform and support of her husband's measures.

After his death, Mrs. Roosevelt was made a delegate to the United Nations General Assembly, one of the few women to be so honored. President Truman also appointed her as United States member of the Human Rights Commission of the United Nations Economic and Social Council.

Bess Wallace Truman

She resigned as United Nations delegate in 1953, at the close of the Truman administration, but as a private citizen continued her work for the world organization. As founder and member of the board of the American Association for the United Nations she toured the country, enlisting support for the U.N. In addition to this as her principal activity, she continued to write, lecture, and travel on behalf of other causes.

On October 11, 1959, her 75th birthday, Mrs. Roosevelt received tributes from all over the world, and was hailed as "a living institution and one of the best-known women in the world."

Mrs. Roosevelt died on November 7, 1962, in New York City.

Truman's Administration

Elizabeth Virginia (Bess) Wallace Truman was born in Independence, Mo., on February 13, 1885, daughter of Madge (Gates) and David Willock Wallace. She and her future husband were graduated from Independence High School in the same class of 1901. From 1904 to 1906 she attended Miss Barstow's School for Girls in Kansas City, Mo., specializing in literature and languages. She became engaged to Harry Truman in 1917. They were married on June 28, 1919, shortly after Major Truman's discharge from the Army.

In addition to making a home for her husband and daughter (Mary) Margaret, born Feb. 17, 1924, Mrs. Truman shared her husband's work and interests. When he was elected to the U.S. Senate in 1934, she became his secretary. Later, as First Lady of the Land, she accepted her social duties graciously but continued as far as possible the family's former quiet home life.

Mamie Geneva Doud Eisenhower

Margaret Truman, who became Mrs. Clifton Daniel, Jr., on April 21, 1956, made her professional debut as a singer in 1947. Mrs. Truman died October 18, 1982.

Eisenhower's Administration

Mamie Geneva Doud Eisenhower was born in Boone, Iowa, on Nov. 14, 1896, daughter of John Sheldon Doud, a prosperous meat packer who retired to Denver in 1905. She attended Denver public schools and also Miss Walcott's. During a family visit to San Antonio, in 1915, she met Second Lieutenant Eisenhower at Fort Sam Houston. They were married in July 1916, and set up housekeeping in quarters at the post.

Army assignments had taken Mrs. Eisenhower with her husband to many parts of the world before she became First Lady in 1953. They were stationed in the Panama Canal Zone, the Philippines, in Europe, and at numerous Army posts in the United States. Their white farmhouse in Gettysburg, Pa., became their first permanent home.

In the White House, Mrs. Eisenhower consistently avoided the spotlight. However, her wide experience as a famous soldier's wife, her personal charm, and her happy facility for getting along with people amply qualified her for meeting the social demands made on the nation's First Lady.

The Eisenhower's first child, Dwight, died at three of scarlet fever. Their second, John Sheldon Doud Eisenhower, was born in 1923, graduated from West Point in 1944 and in 1947 married Barbara Jean Thompson. Their children are Dwight David, Barbara Anne, Susan Elaine, and Mary Jean.

Jacqueline Lee Bouvier Kennedy

KENNEDY'S ADMINISTRATION

Jacqueline Lee Bouvier Kennedy was born July 28, 1929, in Southhampton, Long Island, daughter of the late John V. Bouvier III, New York broker, and Janet (Lee) Bouvier, now Mrs. Hugh D. Auchincloss. She was voted the Most Beautiful Debutante of 1948.

After attending Miss Porter's School in Farmington, Conn., Jacqueline Bouvier went to Vassar for two years, then spent a year at the Sorbonne in Paris. Winning Vogue's Prix de Paris for excellence in design and editorial ability, she could have had another year in Paris, but returned to live with her mother and stepfather in McLean, Va., while completing her work for the B.A. degree which she received in 1951.

Jacqueline Bouvier was the Inquiring Camera Girl (a combination photographer-reporter job) for the Washington Times-Herald at the time she and Senator Kennedy were introduced. On September 12, 1953, they were married at St. Mary's Church in Newport R.I., Archbishop Richard J. Cushing officiating.

A youthful First Lady, Mrs. Kennedy was especially interested in restoring and preserving the character of the public rooms of the White House. She was responsible for redecorating rooms and bringing in furniture and paintings to enhance the historic atmosphere of the Executive Mansion. Mrs. Kennedy accompanied her husband on several important trips to foreign countries and meetings, charming heads of state. Her ability to speak to the peoples of foreign countries in their native tongues won their affection.

Jacqueline Kennedy was appointed by President Johnson to the Committee for the Preservation of the White House, continuing the work she began as First Lady.

Claudia Alta Taylor Johnson

LYNDON JOHNSON'S ADMINISTRATION

Claudia Alta Taylor Johnson was born on December 22, 1912, in Karnack, Texas, daughter of Thomas Jefferson Taylor, businessman and farmer, and Minnie Patillo Taylor. She acquired the nickname "Lady Bird" as a child.

Claudia Taylor went to elementary school in Fern, Texas, and was graduated from Marshall High School, Texas in 1928 at the age of 15. She then attended St. Mary's Episcopal School for Girls in Dallas, graduating in 1930. She was awarded a Bachelor of Arts degree from the University of Texas in 1933, earning a Bachelor of Journalism degree a year later. After a brief courtship, she and Lyndon Johnson were married on November 17, 1934.

Mrs. Johnson received an inheritance from her mother's estate, and the future First Lady invested it by purchasing a radio station in Austin, Texas. In time this became a very profitable operation and demonstrated Mrs. Johnson's business ability. She resigned as chairman of the board of the company when her husband succeeded to the Presidency, and control was transferred to a trusteeship.

An accomplished amateur decorator, Mrs. Johnson decorated and furnished the 100-year-old, 13-room home on the Johnsons' 480-acre ranch 65 miles from Austin.

Mrs. Johnson traveled with her husband on numerous campaign trips and journeys abroad on behalf of the government while he was Vice President. They visited 33 countries and traveled 120,000 miles in foreign lands. A feature of her more than five years as First Lady was her devotion to conservation and to beautifying America. She traveled widely throughout the country.

Thelma Catherine Patricia Ryan Nixon

NIXON'S ADMINISTRATION

Thelma Catherine Patricia Ryan Nixon was born in Ely, Nevada, on March 16, 1912, daughter of William and Kate Halberstadt Ryan. A year later, the family moved to California.

Pat Ryan went to school in Artesia and attended the Community Methodist Church there. She was graduated cum laude from the University of Southern California, became a teacher at Whittier High School and met Mr. Nixon, all in 1937.

Before going to college, Pat Ryan worked as an X-ray technician in New York City to earn education money. During her college years she did research, graded papers, played movie bit parts and worked Saturdays and vacations in department stores.

The Nixons were married in a Quaker ceremony on June 21, 1940, at the Mission Inn, Riverside, California.

While Mr. Nixon was in military service during World War II, Mrs. Nixon accompanied him whenever possible. When he was stationed at Ottumwa, Iowa, she worked there as a bank teller, and later as a government economist in Washington and San Francisco when he was in the South Pacific. They were together in Philadelphia, Baltimore and New York and were living in Baltimore in 1945 when Mr. Nixon was suggested as a Congressional candidate from California.

Mrs. Nixon traveled more than 141,000 air miles with her husband when he was Vice President and went on goodwill missions to 52 countries. In addition, she traveled extensively during campaigns for the presidency.

Elizabeth Bloomer Ford

Elizabeth Bloomer Ford was born on April 8, 1918, in Chicago, Ill. Her marriage to Gerald Ford is her second.

She graduated from Central High School in 1936 and attended the Bennington School of Dance in Vermont for two years. She became a member of the Martha Graham concert group. In Grand Rapids, she organized her own dance group and was also a model and department store fashion coordinator.

Elizabeth Bloomer married Gerald Ford on Oct. 15, 1948, a few weeks before he was elected to his first term as U.S. Representative from the Fifth District of Michigan.

The Fords have four children. Michael Gerald was born in 1950 and married to Gayle Brumbaugh in July, 1974. John Gardner was born in 1952, Steven Meigs in 1956, and Susan Elizabeth in 1957.

An active sports participant, Mrs. Ford likes to ski and swim. She is also an avid gardener.

During her more than a quarter-century as the wife of a Congressman, Vice President and President, Mrs. Ford has joined numerous Republican activities with the Congressional Wives Club, Congressional Club and Republican Wives Club.

Mrs. Ford was a very popular First Lady. She was candid in interviews and presented the picture of being mother and wife in a typical American family.

President Ford called her the spokesman for the family. She was also considered an excellent campaigner.

Rosalynn Smith Carter

CARTER'S ADMINISTRATION

Rosalynn Smith Carter was born on August 18, 1927 in Plains, Ga., daughter of Edgar and Allie Smith. Her family, like her husband's, has lived in the Plains area for more than two centuries.

Rosalynn Smith's father was a garage mechanic who died when she was only 13 years old, leaving a widow and four children. Rosalynn's mother worked in a post office, took in sewing and made bridal trousseaus to earn a living for the family. Rosalynn was a beautician.

The Carters, acquaintances for years, first dated in 1944 when he was home on a weekend from the Naval Academy. They were married two years later. She has noted that the first date made her decide to want to marry Jimmy.

Mrs. Carter worked hard for her husband on both his presidential campaigns, and together with other family members traveled extensively to speak on his behalf.

As First Lady, she was a close political confidant of the President. She frequently advised him and sat in on cabinet meetings.

Mrs. Carter actively promoted mental health and day-care center programs. She occasionally represented the United States at official functions abroad, and was a gracious White House hostess.

Nancy Davis Reagan

Reagan's Administration

Nancy Davis Reagan was born on July 6, 1921 in New York, the only daughter of Dr. and Mrs. Loyal Davis. Her brother, Dr. Richard Davis, is a neurosurgeon.

Nancy Davis grew up in Chicago where she was graduated from Girl's Latin School. She is also a graduate of Smith College, Northhampton, Mass.

She was an actress who met her husband when he, as president of the Screen Actors Guild, helped her clear her name from a similar one on rosters of communist-front groups. The Reagans were married in 1952.

During the period her husband was governor of California, Nancy Reagan visited wounded Vietnam veterans. She was also a regular visitor at hospitals and homes for senior citizens and schools for physically and emotionally handicapped children.

Mrs. Reagan has been especially enamoured with the Foster Grandparent Program, a project that brings together senior citizens and handicapped children. She was to be active in this as First Lady.

She is a former honorary national chairman of Aid to Adoption of Special Kids, and has been active in projects for servicemen who have been taken prisoner and who were missing in action in Vietnam.

Good Housekeeping Magazine honored Mrs. Reagan as one of the 10 most admired women in the nation. She has also been honored by the Disabled American Veterans.

A dedicated supporter of her husband during his years of political campaigning, Mrs. Reagan frequently appeared with him on the platform when he spoke.

Barbara Pierce Bush

BUSH'S ADMINISTRATION

Barbara Pierce Bush was born on June 8, 1925, daughter of Marvin and Pauline Pierce. Her father was the publisher of Redbook and McCall's magazines.

Mrs. Bush was a student at Smith College and has received honorary degrees from Stritch College, Mt. Vernon College, Hood College, and Howard University.

She has dedicated her public life to literacy, belonging to numerous organizations, such as The Council for Effective Literacy, and volunteering her time to help the underprivileged become literate.

She married George Bush on January 6, 1945, in Rye, New York; both are Episcopalian. The Bushes have five children: George Walker, John Ellis, Neil Mallon, Marvin Pierce, and Dorothy Walker. Their sixth child, Robin, died of leukemia in 1953.

The Bushes have been married for forty-eight years, and have lived in twenty-six homes, including the White House.

Hillary Diane Rodham Clinton

CLINTON'S ADMINISTRATION

Hillary Diane Rodham Clinton was born in Chicago, Illinois, in October of 1947 to Hugh and Dorothy Howell Rodham. Mrs. Clinton has two younger brothers, Hugh and Tony.

Mrs. Clinton graduated from Wellesley College in 1969 and received her law degree from Yale in 1973. While at Yale she met Bill Clinton and they were married in 1975. They have a daughter, Chelsea, who was born in 1980.

As the Governor's wife in Arkansas, Mrs. Clinton was and is a committed leader for families and children. She founded the Arkansas Advocates for Children and Families. She has served on the Board of the Children's Defense Fund, Children's Television Workshop, the National Center on Education and the Economy and the Child Action Campaign. Mrs. Clinton has twice been named as one of "The 100 Most Influential Lawyers in America" by the National Law Journal.

Within the first 30 days of his administration The President appointed the First Lady as Chairperson of the Health Care Task Force. Mrs. Clinton has taken this appointment as the First Lady, without pay.

Wives of the Presidents

PRESIDENT	Date of Marriage	Wife's Name	Born-Died	State Where Born
George Washington	1759	Martha (Dandridge) Custis	1731-1802	VA
John Adams	1764	Abigail Smith	1744-1818	MA
Thomas Jefferson	1772	Martha (Wayles) Skelton	1748-1782	VA
James Madison	1794	Dorothy ("Dolley") (Payne) Todd	1772-1849	NC
James Monroe	1786	Eliza Kortright	1768-1830	NY
John Quincy Adams	1797	Louisa Catherine Johnson	1775-1852	England
Andrew Jackson	1791	Rachel (Donelson) Robards	1767-1828	VA
Martin Van Buren	1807	Hannah Hoes	1783-1819	NY
William Henry Harrison	1795	Anna Symmes	1775-1864	NJ
John Tyler	1813	Letitia Christian	1790-1842	VA
	1844	Julia Carginer	1820-1889	NY
James Polk	1824	Sarah Childress	1803-1891	TN
Zachary Taylor	1810	Margaret Smith	1788-1852	MD
Millard Fillmore	1826	Abigail Powers	1798-1853	NY
	1858	Caroline (Carmichael) McIntosh	1813-1881	NJ
Franklin Pierce	1834	Jane Means Appleton	1806-1863	NH
James Buchanan		Unmarried		
Abraham Lincoln	1842	Mary Todd	1818-1882	KY
Andrew Johnson	1827	Eliza McCardle	1810-1876	TN
Ulysses Simpson Grant	1848	Julia Dent	1826-1902	MO
Rutherford Birchard Hayes	1852	Lucy Ware Webb	1831-1889	OH
James Abram Garfield	1858	Lucretia Rudolph	1832-1918	OH
Chester Alan Arthur	1859	Ellen Lewis Herndon	1837-1880	VA
Grover Cleveland	1886	Frances Folsom	1864-1947	NY
Benjamin Harrison	1853	Caroline Lavinia Scott	1832-1892	OH
	1896	Mary Scott (Lord) Dimmick	1858-1948	PA
William McKinley	1871	Ida Saxton	1847-1907	OH
Theodore Roosevelt	1880	Alice Hathaway Lee	1861-1884	MA
	1886	Edith Kermit Carow	1861-1948	NY
William Howard Taft	1886	Helen Herron	1861-1943	OH
Woodrow Wilson	1885	Ellen Louise Axson	1860-1914	GA
	1915	Edith (Bolling) Galt	1872-1961	VA
Warren Gamaliel Harding	1891	Florence Kling	1860-1924	OH
Calvin Coolidge	1905	Grace Anna Goodhue	1879-1957	VT
Herbert Clark Hoover	1899	Lou Henry	1875-1944	IA
Franklin Delano Roosevelt	1905	Anna Eleanor Roosevelt	1884-1962	NY
Harry S. Truman	1919	Elizabeth Virginia Wallace	1885-1982	MO
Dwight David Eisenhower	1916	Mamie Geneva Doud	1896-1979	IA
John Fitzgerald Kennedy	1953	Jacqueline Lee Bouvier	1929-	NY
Lyndon Baines Johnson	1934	Claudia Alta Taylor	1912-	TX
Richard Milhous Nixon	1940	Thelma Catherine Patricia Ryan	1912-	NV
Gerald Rudolph Ford	1940	Elizabeth Bloomer	1918-	IL
James Earl Carter	1946	Rosalynn Smith	1927-	GA
Ronald Wilson Reagan	1952	Nancy Davis	1921-	NY
George Herbert Walker Bush	1945	Barbara Pierce	1925-	NY
William Jefferson Clinton	1975	Hillary Diane Rodham	1947-	IL

The WHITE HOUSE

For more than a century and a half, the White House has been the home of the Presidents of the United States. It has been the scene of many brilliant social affairs—weddings, fetes, receptions—and also of sorrowful events. Like the nation itself, it bears the imprint of successive chief executives. Designed originally to avoid formal display, it has an air of dignity and charm. Now rebuilt to last for centuries, the White House retains the simplicity of its original appearance and its rich historical associations.

The cornerstone of the White House, the first public building to be erected in Washington, was laid on October 13, 1792. President Washington selected the site, which was included on the plan of the Federal City prepared by the French engineer, Maj. Pierre L'Enfant. The plans for the house, approved by Washington, were drawn by James Hoban, an Irish-born architect. Hoban superintended the construction of the house, its rebuilding after burning by British forces in 1814, and the erection of the north and south porticos some years later.

In the classical style of architecture, the main facade of the White House resembles the Duke of Leinster's house in Dublin, on which the design was supposedly based. Details of other faces and the interior arrangement were probably derived from contemporary houses in England and Europe. Built of sandstone quarried on Aquia Creek, VA., the exterior walls were painted during the course of construction, causing the building to be termed the "White House" from an early date. For many years, however, it was generally referred to as the "President's House" or the "President's Palace."

Early History

The White House was first occupied by President and Mrs. John Adams in November 1800. Some of its interior had not then been completed and Mrs. Adams used the unfinished East Room to dry the family wash. During Jefferson's administration, the east and west terraces were contructed. Jefferson practiced democratic simplicity in his social life, and it was his custom to open the house each morning to all arrivals. When James Madison became President in 1809, his wife, the famous Dolley Madison, introduced some of the brilliance and glitter of old-world courts into the social life of the White House. Then, on August 24, 1814, British forces captured Washington and burned the building in retaliation for the destruction by American troops of some public buildings in

Canada. Although only the partially damaged sandstone walls and the interior brickwork remained when the work of reconstruction was begun in the spring of 1815, the building was ready for occupancy by President Monroe in December 1817. The south portico, the dominant architectural feature of that side of the house, was built in 1824 and the large north portico over the entrance and driveway, in 1829.

Improvements, 1830-1902

Throughout its history the White House has kept pace with modern improvements. Spring water was piped into the building in 1834, and gas lighting was introduced in 1848. A hot water heating system was installed 5 years later. During Andrew Johnson's administration, the east terrace was entirely removed. In 1882, the first elevator was put in, and the house was wired for electricity a decade later, during the administration of Benjamin Harrison.

Restoration of 1902

No other important structural changes were made in the house until 1902, during the Theodore Roosevelt administration. By this date the interior of the house had become something of a conglomeration of styles and periods because of the many changes made at various times in decorations and arrangements. The house was also badly in need of extensive structural repairs. To correct these conditions, Congress appropriated more than half a million dollars to repair and refurnish the house and to construct new offices for the President. Work was begun in June 1902 by McKim, Meade and White, architects from New York, and was virtually finished by the end of the year. The improvements included rebuilding and strengthening much of the interior of the house, redecorating and refurnishing the entire main floor, removing the main stairway from the west end of the corridor to the east of the entrance lobby and using the space thus made available for enlarging the State Dining Room, providing a few rooms for servants in the attic, erecting an office building at the end of the west terrace, and reconstructing the east terrace.

Alterations, 1903-48

Few important changes were made in the White House during this period. The Executive Office building was enlarged in 1910, several guest rooms were made in the attic during President Wilson's administration, and the roof and third story were remodeled in 1927. Early in the administration of Franklin D. Roosevelt funds were raised by public subscription for the construction of a swimming pool. A few years later a modern electric kitchen was installed, and a basement was dug under the north portico to provide space for maintenance shops and storage. World War II saw an air raid shelter constructed off the new East Wing, a motion picture theater put in under the east terrace, and a small gymnasium set up adjoining the swimming pool. In 1946, a balcony was built off the second floor, behind the columns of the south portico, to provide a porch for the President's family and also to improve the appearance of the portico, the columns of which appeared too tall and slender for such an important architectural feature.

White House Renovation, 1948-52

Over the years, piecemeal alterations had weakened many of the old wooden beams and interior walls, but not until a thorough examination of the structure was made in 1948 was the really alarming condition of the house revealed. Beams were found to be inadequately supported, heavy ceilings had dropped several inches, even the foundations were found too weak to support the walls erected on them. Consequently, a Commission on Renovation of the Executive Mansion was established, according to an act of Congress approved April 14, 1949, to decide whether to erect an entirely new building or preserve as much as possible of the old structure. After careful consideration, the Commission decided that the old sandstone walls would be retained, thus preserving the historical appearance of the famous old structure.

So that preliminary surveys could be made, President Truman and his family moved across the street into the historic Blair House, and all of the furnishings were removed and placed in storage in December 1948. The actual work of reconstruction was begun a year later, and by the fall of 1950 the most critical phase of the work had been accomplished. The old walls were now supported by concrete foundations, and the wooden beams and brick supporting walls of the interior were replaced by a modern steel framework. Concrete floors were then laid and partition walls erected.

Space for electrical and refrigeration equipment was provided by excavating an area northeast of the White House. A new floor and steps for the north portico were constructed of Tennessee marble. Georgia marble was used for the floor of the south portico and Missouri limestone for the steps.

During 1951, the exterior was painted white, walls and ceilings were plastered, and the interior woodwork was installed.

In addition to making the White House as fireproof and durable as possible, every effort was made during the renovation to retain or restore the original atmosphere and at the same time to provide a more livable and efficient home for the President and his family. Where there were formerly 48 rooms and 14 baths in the part of the house used as living quarters, there were now 54 rooms and 16 baths. In all, the White House today has 132 rooms and 20 baths and showers, compared with 62 rooms and 14 baths prior to the renovation. Formerly, there was but one elevator, now there are five—a main elevator, a service elevator, and three freight elevators. Altogether, Congress appropriated $5,761,000 for the renovation, which was scheduled to be completed in 1951, but various difficulties delayed its completion. President Truman and his family resumed residence in the White House on March 27, 1952.

The First Floor

In general, furnishings and decorations are predominantly eighteenth-century Georgian in style, but furnishings of historic interest have been retained; much of the old furniture has been refinished and recovered to harmonize with the color scheme of various rooms. Some of the new furnishings were given by anonymous donors.

Entrance Lobby and Main Corridor

Six classic columns separate the entrance lobby from the main corridor. The columns and the pilasters spaced along the walls are of varicolored Vermont marble; floors are of gray and pink Tennessee marble. The entrance to the main stairway, which was formerly from the corridor, is now from the east side of the lobby. Seals of the Thirteen Original States are carved on the marble-faced opening of the stairway.

The President's office is oval and was added in 1909 to the West Wing. It looks out on the Rose Garden.

The East Room

Used for state receptions and balls, the East Room is the largest room in the White House. It has been the scene of several famous weddings, including those of Nellie Grant and Alice Roosevelt. Funeral services were held here for William Henry Harrison, Zachary Taylor, Abraham Lincoln, Warren G. Harding, and Franklin D. Roosevelt.

The East Room is decorated in white and gold. Window draperies are of lemon-gold and white silk damask. White enameled wood paneling covers the walls, in which are set six low-relief panels done in 1902 by Piccirilli Brothers. The large crystal chandeliers hanging from an elaborately decorated plaster ceiling also date from 1902. The floor is oak parquetry. On the east wall is seen the most notable portrait in the White House - that of George Washington painted by Gilbert Stuart. It is the one Dolley Madison ordered removed when the British burned the White House in 1814. A portrait of Martha Washington also hangs on the east wall.

The Green Room

This room is used for informal receptions. The walls are covered with green silk damask, and the draperies are of the same material. The white marble mantel, imported from Italy when the White House was rebuilt after the War of 1812, was originally in the State Dining Room. The Hannibal clock and gilt vases on the mantel were purchased in France during Monroe's administration. On the oak floor is a Savonnerie rug bearing the President's seal in its center.

The Blue Room

Famous for its elliptical shape, this room has usually been considered the most beautiful room in the White House. The walls above the white enameled wainscoting are covered with bright blue silk damask with a gold motif. Draperies and upholstery are of the same material. The furniture is white, matching the woodwork. The uncovered oak floor is laid in herringbone design. On the white marble mantel, which dates from 1902, are a French Minerva clock and gilt candlesticks purchased by President James Monroe. In this room the President receives guests at state dinners and receptions. Grover Cleveland and Frances Folsom were married in the Blue Room on June 2, 1886, the only wedding of a President to take place in the White House.

The Red Room

The size and shape of the Red Room is identical to the Green Room. It has white enameled wainscoting and woodwork, wall covering and draperies of red silk damask, and a red chenille rug on the oak floor. The white marble mantel is a duplicate of that in the Green Room. On it are two eighteenth century candelabra and a musical clock presented in April 1952 by the President of France. This room is used by the First Lady to receive guests and also as a reception room for small dinners. President Rutherford B. Hayes took his oath of office here on March 3, 1877.

The State Dining Room

Except for the East Room, this is the largest room in the White House and can comfortably seat 100 guests at large dinners or luncheons. Paneling of English oak extends from floor to ceiling.

The Private Dining Room

This room has a vaulted ceiling, white enameled wainscoting, and walls paneled in plaster. To the west is the butler's pantry, which opens also into the State Dining Room and is connected with the kitchen on the ground floor by a servant's elevator, dumb-waiters, and a staircase.

The Second Floor

The second and third floors are reserved for the family and guests of the President. The Lincoln bedroom, in which stands the enormous bed used by the Civil War President, was restored in the Victorian period.

The Third Floor

During the renovation the roof was recovered with green slate and raised at the corners to provide additional rooms on the third floor. There are several guest rooms on this floor, most of them furnished with reproductions of eighteenth-century pieces. A ramp leads to the new sun parlor, or solarium, over the south portico.

The Ground Floor

A corridor with vaulted ceiling and varicolored Vermont marble walls gives access to the rooms on this floor. The library, china room, and cloak rooms are paneled in pine from the old beams of the White House, and, in places, show old nail holes. Across the hall is the original kitchen of the White House in which the old sandstone fireplaces have been restored. Adjoining it is a modern electric kitchen, in which almost all the equipment is of stainless steel.

Basement and Mezzanine

Excavating done in the course of renovation provided these additional floors. Here are the machinery and electrical equipment for heating, lighting, and air conditioning the building, and space for storage and service facilities.

Grounds

The impression of simple dignity conveyed by the White House is enhanced by the natural beauty of its informal but carefully landscaped grounds. Many of the trees are of historical interest, such as the magnolias planted by Andrew Jackson. In front of the north portico, English boxwood, as old as the White House itself, has been planted. New trees have been selected for their beauty and variety. Flower gardens and well-kept lawns add to the beauty of the grounds of the White House.

Visitors

The White House is open to visitors from 10 a.m. to 12 noon, Tuesday through Saturday, except on holidays. It is open to 2 p.m. Saturday from June 1 through Labor Day. Admitted at the east entrance to the ground-floor corridor, visitors ascend the stairway to the main floor and are permitted to view the public rooms.

Fine Arts Project

"To make the White House a museum of our country's heritage and a testimonial to American fine arts and cabinet-making. . ."

With this as her announced purpose, in 1961 Jacqueline Kennedy set in motion a far-reaching project for recreating in the White House a setting of authentic American furnishings of the 1802 era, in which the mansion first reached completion as the President's Home. She appointed a Fine Arts Commission to seek out such furnishings, and a special Committee for White House Paintings to work with the Commission in acquiring 18th and 19th century paintings by American artists.

Early in 1962, in an historic and nationally broadcast televised tour of White House rooms, Mrs. Kennedy "reported to the nation" on the Fine Arts project and pointed out paintings and furnishings thus far acquired by loan or gift. The Fine Arts acquisitions are on view to the thousands of daily visitors who pass through the first floor (public) rooms of the White House.

THE OFFICIAL VICE-PRESIDENTIAL RESIDENCE
OBSERVATORY CIRCLE
WASHINGTON, DC

The Presidents' Parents

Birth and death dates; maiden name of mother; year of marriage

1. Augustine Washington, 1694-1743; Mary Ball, 1708-1789; 1730.
2. John Adams 1691-1761; Susanna Boylston, 1699-1797; 1734.
3. Peter Jefferson, 1708-1757; Jane Randolph, 1720-1776; 1739.
4. James Madison, 1723-1801; Eleanor Rose Conway, 1731-1829; 1749.
5. Spence Monroe, -1774; Eliza Jones, - , 1752.
6. John Adams, 1735-1826; Abigail Smith, 1744-1818; 1764.
7. Andrew Jackson, -1767; Elizabeth Hutchinson, -1780.
8. Abraham Van Buren, 1737-1817; Maria Hoes Van Alen, 1747-1817; 1776
9. Benjamin Harrison, 1726-1791; Elizabeth Bassett, 1730-1792; 1748.
10. John Tyler, 1747-1813; Mary Armistead, 1761-1797; 1776.
11. Samuel Polk, 1772-1827; Jane Knox, 1776-1852; 1794
12. Richard Taylor, 1744-1829; Sarah Strother, 1760-1822; 1779.
13. Nathaniel Fillmore, 1771-1863; Phoebe Millard, 1780-1831; 1796?
14. Benjamin Pierce, 1757-1839; Anna Kendrick, 1768-1838; 1790.
15. James Buchanan, 1761-1821; Elizabeth Speer, 1767-1833; 1788.
16. Thomas Lincoln, 1778-1851; Nancy Hanks, 1784-1818; 1806.
17. Jacob Johnson, 1778-1812; Mary McDonough, 1783-1856; 1801.
18. Jesse Root Grant, 1794-1873; Hannah Simpson, 1798-1883; 1821.
19. Rutherford Hayes, 1787-1822; Sophia Birchard, 1792-1866; 1813.
20. Abram Garfield, 1799-1833; Eliza Ballou, 1801-1888; 1820.
21. William Arthur, 1796-1875; Malvina Stone, 1802-1869; 1821.

22, 24. Richard F. Cleveland, 1804-1853; Anne Neal, 1806-1882; 1829.

23. John Scott Harrison, 1804-1878; Elizabeth Ramsey Irwin, 1810-1850; 1831.
25. William McKinley, 1807-1892; Nancy Campbell Allison, 1809-1897; 1829.
26. Theodore Roosevelt, 1831-1878; Martha Bulloch, 1834-1884; 1853.
27. Alphonso Taft, 1810-1891; Louise Maria Torrey, 1827-1907; 1853.
28. Joseph Ruggles Wilson, 1822-1903; Jessie Janet Woodrow, 1826-1888; 1849.
29. George T. Harding, 1843-1928; Phoebe E. Dickerson, 1843-1910; 1864.
30. John Calvin Coolidge, 1845-1926; Victoria J. Moor, 1846-1885; 1868.
31. Jesse Clark Hoover, 1846-1880; Hulda Randall Minthorn, 1848-1883; 1870.
32. James Roosevelt, 1828-1900; Sara Delano, 1854-1941; 1880.
33. John Anderson Truman, 1851-1914; Martha Ellen Young, 1852-1947; 1881.
34. David Jacob Eisenhower, 1863-1942; Ida Elizabeth Stover, 1862-1946; 1885.
35. Joseph Patrick Kennedy, 1888-1969; Rose Fitzgerald, 1890- ; 1914.
36. Samuel Ealy Johnson, 1877-1936; Rebekah Baines, 1881-1958; 1907.
37. Francis Anthony Nixon, 1879-1956; Hannah Milhous, 1885-1967; 1908.
38. Leslie King Sr., 1882-1941; Dorothy Gardner, 1892-1967.
39. James Earl Carter, 1894-1953; Lillian Gordy, 1898-1984; 1923.
40. John Edward Reagan, 1883-1941; Nelle Wilson, 1883-1962; 1904.
41. Prescott Sheldon Bush, 1895-1972; Dorothy Walker, 1901-1992; 1921.
42. William Jefferson Blyth III, 1918-1946; Virginia Cassidy, 1924- ; 1943.

Additional books
may be purchased by remitting

$ 3.50 plus $ 1.30 postage for each copy.

To:
Richard W. Coffman
1612 Ladd Street
Silver Spring, Maryland 20902